W9-CHR-717

Praise for *Inside the Minds*

"The Inside the Minds series is a valuable probe into the thought, perspectives, and techniques of accomplished professionals…" - Chuck Birenbaum, Partner, Thelen Reid & Priest

"Unlike any other business book." - Bruce Keller, Partner, Debevoise & Plimpton

"A must read for anyone in the industry." - Dr. Chuck Lucier, Chief Growth Officer, Booz-Allen & Hamilton

"A snapshot of everything you need…" - Charles Koob, Co-Head of Litigation Department, Simpson Thacher & Bartlet

"A great way to see across the changing marketing landscape at a time of significant innovation." - David Kenny, Chairman & CEO, Digitas

"An incredible resource of information to help you develop outside-the-box…" - Rich Jernstedt, CEO, Golin/Harris International

"Tremendous insights…" - James Quinn, Litigation Chair, Weil Gotshal & Manges

"Great information for both novices and experts." - Patrick Ennis, Partner, ARCH Venture Partners

"A rare peek behind the curtains and into the minds of the industry's best." - Brandon Baum, Partner, Cooley Godward

"Unique insights into the way the experts think and the lessons they've learned from experience." - MT Rainey, Co-CEO, Young & Rubicam/Rainey Kelly Campbell Roalfe

"Intensely personal, practical advice from seasoned dealmakers." - Mary Ann Jorgenson, Coordinator of Business Practice Area, Squire, Sanders & Dempsey

"Great practical advice and thoughtful insights." - Mark Gruhin, Partner, Schmeltzer, Aptaker & Shepard, P.C.

www.Aspatore.com

Aspatore Books is the largest and most exclusive publisher of C-Level executives (CEO, CFO, CTO, CMO, partner) from the world's most respected companies and law firms. Aspatore annually publishes a select group of C-Level executives from the Global 1,000, top 250 law firms (partners and chairs), and other leading companies of all sizes. C-Level Business Intelligence™, as conceptualized and developed by Aspatore Books, provides professionals of all levels with proven business intelligence from industry insiders – direct and unfiltered insight from those who know it best – as opposed to third-party accounts offered by unknown authors and analysts. Aspatore Books is committed to publishing an innovative line of business and legal books, those which lay forth principles and offer insights that when employed, can have a direct financial impact on the reader's business objectives, whatever they may be. In essence, Aspatore publishes critical tools – need-to-read as opposed to nice-to-read books – for all business professionals.

Inside the Minds

The critically acclaimed *Inside the Minds* series provides readers of all levels with proven business intelligence from C-Level executives (CEO, CFO, CTO, CMO, partner) from the world's most respected companies. Each chapter is comparable to a white paper or essay and is a future-oriented look at where an industry/profession/topic is heading and the most important issues for future success. Each author has been carefully chosen through an exhaustive selection process by the *Inside the Minds* editorial board to write a chapter for this book. *Inside the Minds* was conceived in order to give readers actual insights into the leading minds of business executives worldwide. Because so few books or other publications are actually written by executives in industry, *Inside the Minds* presents an unprecedented look at various industries and professions never before available.

Winning Legal Strategies in Health Care

Leading Lawyers on Industry Regulations &
Creating Legal Game Plans

BOOK IDEA SUBMISSIONS

If you are a C-Level executive or senior lawyer interested in submitting a book idea or manuscript to the Aspatore editorial board, please e-mail jason@aspatore.com. Aspatore is especially looking for highly specific book ideas that would have a direct financial impact on behalf of a reader. Completed books can range from 20 to 2,000 pages – the topic and "need to read" aspect of the material are most important, not the length. Include your book idea, biography, and any additional pertinent information.

Published by Aspatore, Inc.

For corrections, company/title updates, comments, or any other inquiries, please e-mail info@aspatore.com.

First Printing, 2005
10 9 8 7 6 5 4 3 2 1

ISBN 1-58762-964-X Library of Congress Control Number: 2005929650

Inside the Minds Managing Editor, Laura Kearns, Edited by Eddie Fournier, Proofread by Brian Denitzio

Material in this book is for educational purposes only. This book is sold with the understanding that neither any of the authors or the publisher is engaged in rendering legal, accounting, investment, or any other professional service. Neither the publisher nor the authors assume any liability for any errors or omissions or for how this book or its contents are used or interpreted or for any consequences resulting directly or indirectly from the use of this book. For legal advice, please consult your personal lawyer.

This book is printed on acid-free paper.

A special thanks to all the individuals who made this book possible.

The views expressed by the individuals in this book (or the individuals on the cover) do not necessarily reflect the views shared by the companies they are employed by (or the companies mentioned in this book). The employment status and affiliations of authors with the companies referenced are subject to change.

Winning Legal Strategies
in Health Care

Leading Lawyers on Industry Regulations &
Creating Legal Game Plans

CONTENTS

Meeting the Challenges of a Changing Health Care Environment

Kirk J. Nahra
Partner
Wiley Rein & Fielding LLP

The health care industry is constantly changing — through new scientific developments, critical changes to the regulatory structure overlaying the industry, and developments in how individuals and companies pay for health care services. Understanding these new developments — and building an approach that integrates the business, legal, and risk management components of the changing environment — creates enormous challenges for any entity operating in the health care industry. An effective lawyer in this environment must not only understand the laws and regulations, but must also be able to integrate the legal framework into the ongoing business operations of the health care client, both currently and for the future.

Avoiding Legal Problems

My work is primarily oriented toward compliance and counseling. Litigation may emerge from this work, but it is not a desired result, and it is not usually the point at which I get involved. We are trying to develop a smart framework for the business in the first place — allowing the business to do something that complies with all the laws but still does not create problems in terms of operations or business partner relationships. Much of what I do is litigation avoidance. No one likes the litigation process.

Health care companies must constantly deal with new regulatory regimes. The new focus on privacy laws is a good example. It is an area that has been around for years but has recently taken on an unprecedented scope due to new federal privacy laws, creating substantial compliance challenges and operational change. This is an area that poses regulatory, legislative, law enforcement, and publicity risks. In addition, the privacy laws will lead to some litigation. Any time there are so many laws that are applicable to a business, there will be enforcement issues and litigation problems. Having a good planning process and getting legal and business advice up front will reduce those back end problems.

When reviewing a new client's exposure to legal issues in the industry, I need to understand their business. There are countless rules that are relevant to the health care industry, and not all of them are applicable to all parts. Understanding what their business really is and what kind of services they provide, who their customers are, and whether they are involved in government health care programs is critical. If they are not involved in government programs, that cuts out many of the most troubling issues.

When talking with clients, it is important to try to be reasonable and allow them to understand the different choices they can make. Many of the rules that affect the health care industry are confusing and unclear, so people have to try and add a dose of realism to what they are looking at and try to make sense of all the requirements. One of my challenges is to understand my clients' business operations sufficiently so I can not only provide counsel on the full range of legal options, but also advise them on the legal, risk management, and operational implications of the various choices.

To avoid legal problems, you must understand the issue at hand and implement it in a way that is both realistically compliant with the laws and also not overly compliant or overly conservative, such that you cannot achieve your business goals. Compliance is really a question of trying to get the right balance rather than avoiding the issue.

For example, you cannot avoid drug issues if you are in the health care industry. You try to use a control mechanism and develop appropriate operational strategies that factor in the need to deal with the various health care implications of drug treatments in a way that accommodates the changing legal and regulatory environment. You try to be aware of what is going on in the industry. You try to evolve your payment practices so that if companies are inflating some of their prices in certain areas (and there have been lawsuits dealing with that, and the government is pursuing them), you can factor that in to how you pay for the costs. Health care is a business that takes in information from many different sources — new scientific advancements, changes in the employee benefit structure, government health care program changes, legislation and regulations at the federal, state, and local level, as well as a wide range of litigation results that impact health care operations. With all of these sources — many of which may be in conflict — one of the biggest challenges has been trying to integrate all of that information into an effective compliance and risk management approach. This amount of information — and the wide range of minutia present in the regulations and legislation — have made it important to be an expert in many things, and a generalist in virtually everything, so that legal advice can incorporate not only the specific issue at hand, but also the full range of implications created by the intersections of all these developments.

Changes in the Industry

One of the services I can provide to my clients is keeping them updated on current event developments. I send things out many times a week to significant groups of my clients. Even for people in the business, it is hard to stay on top, because it is such a rapidly developing area. There are five areas that I pay particularly close attention to: developments related to privacy and security, health care fraud, benefit structures, regulatory developments at a federal level, and law enforcement investigations concerning health care behavior.

The health care industry is a much more heavily regulated industry than many others. Some of the laws, such as the HIPAA privacy laws, did not exist at all until drafts began to be issued at the tail end of the Clinton administration, for final implementation in April of 2003. Fraud is an area that has far more attention devoted to it now. Twenty years ago, no one was talking about fraud issues. It was a small focus of attention. Drugs are similar. Drug costs, if you go back more than ten years, were a tiny piece of health care costs. They have now become the biggest single component of health care costs, according to some reports.

In the future, cost control and allocation of health care resources will be an area that everyone will be looking at from a policy perspective. Legislators seem to be trying to get their hands on that, and they are tinkering with who gets the benefits, how care is paid for, and how much the government pays. That allocation of economic resources will continue to be tweaked.

The regulatory process has become so difficult and so burdensome that health care companies do spend a significant amount of their time and assets on compliance issues, more than on providing health care services. It would be lovely if we actually had administrative simplification. Instead, the health care industry has spent hundreds of millions of dollars to bring itself into compliance with these "administrative simplification" laws, which are widely viewed in the industry as an oxymoron. Compliance is far too difficult, and people spend far too much time simplifying things. Having effective administrative simplification would create genuine cost savings and improve efficiency.

Most Common Legal Issues

The legal landscape for health care companies continues to shift, and there are many areas my clients need to be aware of.

Health Care Privacy and Security

Privacy and security issues involve a set of compliance rules that health care companies must follow. They affect virtually everything a health care company does — all components of the company.

The HIPAA law, for example, goes back almost ten years and deals with portability of health care coverage. If you leave your job, can you take your health care coverage with you to your new job? As a result of an agreement on that principle, the legislators threw many other things into that law, one of them being a category called "administrative simplification," which has led to three rules that are huge for the health care industry. There is a privacy rule, there is a health care security rule, and there is a rule called "standard transactions," which relates to formats for submitting all the health care claims that go in and all the payments that come back in the health care system. Those three rules have had a huge impact on the health care industry.

The first challenge from a legal standpoint has been to understand what the rules are, as they are new and still evolving. People have had to figure out what the rules say and how to comply with them across their company. They need to figure out where the problems are. In terms of privacy, for the most part, people are at a point where they have done the basics and have probably taken the next step, and now they are dealing with ongoing compliance challenges, auditing of their programs, changes to their business, and enforcement actions.

In order to solve a privacy problem, you have to understand what happened. Because these are new rules, people are still struggling to interpret them in a way that makes sense from a compliance perspective, yet lets people do what they need to on the business side. People have gotten a bit more comfortable over the last year, so there is a little more flexibility and a little less conservatism in trying to balance those issues. The government has not yet become involved in enforcement, so people are still waiting.

There is also the challenge of developing appropriate compliance structures that encompass the full range of relevant privacy laws — not only the HIPAA rules, but also a wide variety of other privacy laws at the state and federal level (and even internationally) that affect how personal information is used, disclosed, and manipulated.

Security involves a different set of regulations, and it is an area in which companies face multiple sets of rules that are not always consistent — and that is a real challenge. It is also an area in which the government has legislated that people follow best practices. Figuring out what those best practices are will be an ongoing challenge for the health care industry.

Health Care Fraud

Everyone is concerned about health care costs, because they continue to go up. Often, health care costs are rising at a rate that exceeds the general rate of inflation or the growth rate of other kinds of expenses. While there are of course many factors to these consistent increases, one of the biggest components that is viewed as preventable, or one of the best ways to cut costs without having to cut benefits, is to cut back on health care fraud.

Industry analysts estimate that more than $100 billion a year is attributable to health care fraud. It is something the government puts a great deal of time and effort into investigating, detecting, and prosecuting. Companies can be perpetrators of this. Health care companies can also be victims of some of this, and it is an issue every health care company must have at the top of its list of concerns, because fraud exists in such a complicated structure. Not only must companies deal with changing health care rules, but payment changes and benefit changes as well. From the health care provider side, developing an effective way to meet all the billing rules is a real challenge. From the payer side, whether it is government or private, figuring out where the fraud problems are and coming up with an effective way to detect and fight them is also a real challenge.

On the provider side, where you are essentially trying to avoid perpetrating fraud, there are compliance programs — and there have been a number of changes in compliance programs recently. The government is really pushing people to reevaluate, strengthen, and upgrade their compliance approaches.

On the payer side, there are many new software solutions, but detecting fraud is basically a question of trying to uncover oddities in your billing patterns. Much more information is coming in electronically these days, and that presents both good news and bad news. The good news is that things go faster. But faster means you may not be looking at the information as much, so you have to have systems that balance efficiency with still trying to spot anomalies.

Drug-Related Issues

Drug costs are the single fastest-growing component of health care costs, and they involve a variety of issues. There are all the new business issues arising because of the new Medicare drug programs from last year. That is something that will be phased in over the next several years, will have an enormous impact on government drug costs, and will have spillover effects on the private sector. There are many cases that involve abusive drugs, overprescription of drugs, overutilization of drugs, and overpricing of drugs. Certain painkillers, for example, are becoming real black market commodities, and real hardcore criminal cases are appearing. There are also more mainstream pricing issues leading to all kinds of cases involving antitrust allegations, patent manipulations, and various other issues related to how drugs are priced.

Everyone is trying to figure out how to realistically cut back on drug expenditures while still getting the health care benefits.

The government is pursuing two dozen fraud cases related to how drug companies have priced their products. There are a number of antitrust cases in which companies are accused of artificially inflating their prices or suppressing generic alternatives. There are patent-related cases involving price protections for drugs. That has been a huge source of litigation over the past couple of years.

Evolving Benefit Structure

Employers and insurers who are paying for health care are looking for ways to slow down cost escalation through changes in how benefits are developed. Whether that means cutting retiree programs or increasing individual patient payment levels on many benefit plans, there are new kinds of spending accounts that come out of the Medicare legislation. They are a way to basically say to most employees that they are going to have their premiums cut, but they will have to pay more at the early stages. It is a different way of paying for health care, and people are looking at a variety of alternatives to control costs. The development of HMOs took place twenty years ago, and that has pretty much worked its way through the system. Now we have to try to slow down our costs further, and we need to look at other ways to do that.

With regard to benefits, we are trying to take a system that exists today and that is working to a point, but not working as well as we want, and figure out how to change it and improve it in the future, both in terms of general cost control and also in terms of having a product to sell that is attractive to our customers. The customers, who are both individuals and companies that are buying insurance for their employees, are looking for people to come in with creative new approaches. Health care insurance is a tough business. The insurance business has to be developed based on data, predictions, and all kinds of boring economics, so being new and creative is a challenge for the industry.

International Issues

Whenever you are doing business abroad, you have to multiply the complexity many times. While much of the health care industry is a local industry (think of your family physician or local hospital), a growing segment of the health care industry must meet the challenges of a global or international environment. Research institutions receive data from all over the world. Pharmaceutical companies market globally, under very different legal regimes. Insurers are looking not only to provide coverage to

American customers traveling abroad, but also to multinational employers with workforce members around the globe, as well as taking the concept of health insurance to other countries. Many companies have offices and employees out of the country, so companies want to be able to do health care business internationally, but the health care programs are so different in so many places. There are some difficult United States rules that really don't have any analog in other parts of the company, but if you have people in other parts of the country, you may be stuck with applying United States laws (such as the HIPAA privacy rule) to individuals across the globe, because a company's base of operations is in the United States.

Compliance .

Corporate compliance programs are back in the news again. Whether because of widespread corporate compliance failures or the recent actions of the United States Sentencing Commission to revise the compliance requirements necessary to receive a sentencing credit for having an effective corporate compliance program, the need for reinvigorating and expanding existing corporate compliance programs has never been more important — or challenging — for companies operating in the health care field. In the wake of a series of high-profile corporate fraud scandals over the last several years, legislators, government regulators, and prosecutors alike have issued pointed and repeated calls for corporations to adopt more stringent corporate governance codes and policies to ensure greater corporate accountability. Often framed as suggested or recommended "best practices" that corporations could voluntarily accept or decline to implement, a new set of legal principles is creating new imperatives to beef up corporate compliance programs at all levels.

Unlike the initial sentencing guidelines for corporate organizations — which are widely credited with having started a nationwide focus on corporate compliance by providing corporations with specific incentives in the criminal process to develop and maintain effective compliance programs — these new principles focus not only on sentencing issues (although the sentencing impacts remain substantial), but also on the prosecutorial decisions about whether or not to charge corporations with wrongdoing in the first place. These developments reach further beyond the criminal process by focusing attention, particularly for regulated industries facing potential exposure under the False Claims Act, on whether failure to adopt and implement an effective corporate compliance program can itself create civil liability for submitting false claims.

The overall impact of these collective inducements and incentives to focus on corporate compliance efforts has created enormous internal and external pressures for all companies to adopt new, or evaluate existing, compliance programs to better prevent and detect violations of law and avoid or reduce criminal and civil liability. For companies in the health care industry and other industries heavily regulated by the government, the time for action is now, before a failure to improve a corporate compliance program results in significant liabilities for the company. If nothing else, the continuing efforts by government regulators to place a premium on effective compliance programs provides senior managers with assurances that their efforts to examine the scope, strength, and overall effectiveness of their existing compliance program will be rewarded in a tangible, meaningful way.

Accordingly, for compliance professionals and the health care industry as a whole (as well as for any regulated industry facing the possibility of civil and criminal investigations), these recent legal developments constitute a compliance "perfect storm," where companies must fundamentally reevaluate — and reinvigorate — their compliance programs across their operations. These developments are substantial and demonstrate, in the wake of the wide range of recent corporate scandals, a prosecutorial inclination to mandate ethical and compliant corporate behavior, and to reward those who have the right corporate culture and punish those who do not.

With this background, what are the core conclusions that companies should be drawing from these related developments?

- *Ethics in Addition to Compliance*

First, the government is focusing attention on ethics as well as formal legal compliance. Throughout its amendments, the Sentencing Commission added the idea of "ethics" to every reference to a compliance program (therefore requiring a "compliance and ethics program" throughout the amendments). A health care company must ask itself: Does our compliance program incorporate an ethics component? How do we mandate ethical behavior across a company? While there clearly are ambiguities, companies must focus not only on teaching employees how to follow the rules, but also why to follow the rules.

• *Corporate Culture*

The Advisory Group of the Sentencing Commission, which issued a series of important recommendations related to compliance programs, was quite clear — it recommended the changes to the sentencing guidelines to add "a specific requirement that organizations seek to develop a culture in which compliance with the law is the expected behavior." This "cultural" component of compliance programs is pervasive in the Sentencing Commission reports. The culture must stem from corporate management, and it must apply to the full range of activities that intersect with compliance — corporate communications, training, mitigation of problems, business judgments, and the like.

• *Look Beyond Criminal Conduct*

While the final Sentencing Commission amendments removed some references to problematic corporate behavior outside of the criminal process, it is clear that organizations should focus attention beyond criminal violations. A corporate culture that aggressively monitors criminal behavior — but that places a reduced emphasis on compliance with other laws — will not survive scrutiny in the long run.

• *Management Oversight*

Beyond these cultural elements, the other primary emphasis of these interrelated developments is the importance of senior management in developing and monitoring compliance and ethics programs. These programs must be developed and overseen at the highest levels of the company. Because of Sarbanes-Oxley and the Sentencing Commission guidelines, the chief executive officer/chief financial officer should care about the company's compliance program. The board of directors must also play an active role in how the organization follows the law. Accordingly, it is critical for senior management and corporate boards (who also face their own additional pressures under Sarbanes-Oxley) to be involved in the development, maintenance, and ongoing oversight of the compliance program.

- *The Importance of Reporting and Cooperation*

Cooperation with government investigators is also critical. While the Sentencing Commission backed away from a requirement of waiver of attorney-client privilege, it is clear that aggressive cooperation is a component of how government prosecutors and courts will evaluate cooperation. While it also remains feasible for organizations to conduct their own internal investigations, these investigations must be thorough and prompt, and the results should be communicated to government investigators at the earliest appropriate time. A failure to meet these cooperation expectations can essentially eliminate all of the positive value derived from an effective compliance program. And without this cooperation, a compliance and ethics program simply is not effective.

- *Ongoing Reevaluation*

Finally, companies must reevaluate their compliance and ethics programs — constantly. These programs are not pieces of paper that lie on a shelf gathering dust. They must be works in progress — all the time. Whether it is reevaluating the nature of the risk faced by a particular company, auditing the effectiveness of the program, or recognizing that external or internal changes require new compliance efforts, compliance programs are envisioned as a living and breathing part of ongoing corporate operations.

A further component of this ongoing evaluation requires that the compliance and ethics program be staffed appropriately — and that the senior officials in charge of compliance have sufficient resources to do the job properly. This is not an area for cutbacks in staff and budget. In order to oversee a compliance program effectively, and to conduct the kind of ongoing audit and evaluation that is expected by the government, strong staffing levels are critical.

While all of these developments are quite important, and reflect a renewed focus within the government as to the importance of compliance and ethics programs across corporate America, they should also serve as a wakeup call for organizations of all shapes and sizes. Those companies in heavily regulated industries — such as the health care industry — face additional challenges. And while these changes are evolutionary, organizations should take these opportunities to conduct a thorough review of compliance and ethics activities, and to reinvigorate a process that requires constant attention.

Mr. Kirk J. Nahra is a partner with Wiley Rein & Fielding LLP in Washington, D.C., where he specializes in health care, privacy, information security, and insurance fraud litigation and counseling for the health care and property/casualty insurance industries and others facing compliance obligations on these issues. He is chair of the firm's privacy practice and co-chair of its health care practice. He also works with insurers and health care industry participants in developing compliance programs and defending against government investigations into their practices. He assists companies in a wide range of industries with analyzing and implementing the requirements of privacy and security laws across the country and internationally. He was elected to the board of directors of the International Association of Privacy Professionals and serves as the editor of Privacy Officers Advisor, *the monthly newsletter of the International Association of Privacy Professionals.*

Mr. Nahra received his law degree from Harvard Law School, cum laude, in 1987. At Harvard, he served as the articles editor of the Harvard Journal on Legislation. *He received his undergraduate degree from Georgetown University, magna cum laude and Phi Beta Kappa, in 1984.*

*Mr. Nahra is an active author and lecturer in the health care, privacy, and anti-fraud areas. His most recent publications include: "Financial Institutions and the New HIPAA Rules," * The Review of Banking and Financial Services *(June, 2004); "The New Incentives for Enhanced Compliance Programs," * BNA Health Law Reporter *(May 27, 2004); "What's Up with California?"* BNA Privacy and Security Law Report *(January 19, 2004); "Health care Privacy Rules Carry Potential for Lawsuit,"* Washington Business Journal *(December 19, 2003); "Making Sense of HIPAA Privacy for U.S. Employers,"* World Data Protection Report *(September, 2003); and "Getting a Handle on the New HIPAA Security Regulation,"* Privacy Laws and Business International Newsletters *(March/April, 2003).*

Strategic Approaches to Medicaid

Deborah Bachrach
Co-Chair, Not-for-Profit Practice Group

Melinda Dutton
Counsel & Director of Health Care Policy

Manatt, Phelps & Phillips LLP

Background

Medicaid is the nation's largest health insurance program, covering over 53 million Americans and spending over $300 billion annually. It was the largest expenditure in twenty-one state budgets in 2003 (including federal contributions), second only to education in most others. For example, New York State spending on Medicaid was 28.4 percent of total state expenditures in fiscal year 2003, compared to 20.3 percent for elementary and secondary education. In the same year, California spent 18.5 percent, and Tennessee and Missouri both spent approximately a third of total state expenditures on Medicaid.

For low-income consumers, Medicaid means health insurance and access to essential health care services. For health care companies, whether nonprofit or for-profit, management organizations, service providers, or product manufacturers, Medicaid is a revenue stream. For some, it is the single most important revenue stream. Nationally, Medicaid funds 17 percent of hospital care, 12 percent of professional services, 46 percent of nursing home care, and 19 percent of prescription drugs.

For all of these entities, the first challenge in developing a sound Medicaid business strategy is to understand the rules of the Medicaid program in the state or states in which they operate, and to cross-walk those rules with company policies and practices, where necessary modifying practices to comply with state laws and take advantage of state-specific reimbursement opportunities. The bigger challenge is to influence the interpretation of those rules to permit the organization to grow its business, advance its mission, and increase its revenue. It is this challenge on which we focus here.

We work with a wide range of health care companies, from small nonprofit health care organizations to large academic medical centers, to startup ventures, to publicly traded companies. The common theme that emerges is how to ensure an adequate flow of Medicaid dollars, or more specifically, how to ensure that particular services or products are covered by the state's Medicaid program, and that the level of reimbursement approximates the relevant costs. While the details of our strategic advice differs depending on the client's business and the specific problem, the core elements are the same — blending law, politics, and policy.

The Context: The Unique Attributes and Challenges of Medicaid

Before we turn to strategies to influence Medicaid's operating rules, we want to touch on some of the confounding features of the Medicaid program. Unlike Medicare, which is wholly federally funded and regulated, Medicaid is funded by both federal and state dollars. Federal matching rates (the percent of every Medicaid dollar that is covered by federal funds) vary from state to state, from a high of 77 percent in Mississippi to a low of 50 percent in several states, including New York and California. The dual funding streams means Medicaid is vulnerable to both federal and state budget pressures. As a result, there is little predictability from year to year as to reimbursement levels, and there is no certainty that upfront investments will be recouped in the short run or even the long run.

Again, unlike Medicare, Medicaid is regulated by both federal and state law. Federal law and federal regulators set the broad parameters, and state law and state regulators fill in the operating details, including defining the eligible population, covered services, and the rate setting methodology. Federal law can provide protections from some arbitrary state actions, and federal regulators can and increasingly do bar reimbursement mechanisms they view as gimmicks to simply draw down federal matching dollars. In general, however, the state is the focus of key programmatic decision making, and program features, rules, and procedures vary significantly across the nation. This poses particular challenges for providers and businesses operating in multiple states.

Finally, and again in contrast to Medicare, Medicaid is a means-tested program targeted at low-income families and disabled adults. Eligibility for Medicare is fairly straightforward and ongoing, generally based on age (over sixty-five) and work history. Medicaid eligibility is tied to state-defined levels of income and assets, and requires that beneficiaries establish their eligibility at least annually. States are given enormous latitude to decide who is eligible and how eligible populations become and stay enrolled in the program. As a result, the number of beneficiaries is variable, and Medicaid reimbursement for services provided or products sold is never a certainty.

In short, Medicaid is not an easy business partner. A successful business relationship with the Medicaid program requires not only an understanding of its various moving parts, but also a strategy to influence their movement.

Overview of Strategy

The nature of the Medicaid program — an intensely regulated, joint state/federal program — has led to a rich and constantly evolving legal framework that governs virtually every aspect of the program's operation. State and federal statutes and regulations are voluminous and complex, leading to equally voluminous case law and administrative rulings. Yet, it would be a mistake to view the program exclusively or even primarily through a legal lens. The practical operations of Medicaid programs are determined as much by the regulatory bodies — especially state regulatory bodies, but also federal — that govern them as the laws themselves. Medicaid is also the subject of intense political scrutiny; a diverse range of stakeholders who rely on the program for revenue, jobs, or care compete to influence the program's implementation. At the same time, Medicaid is an ideological lightening rod, increasingly under attack for its growth and replacing welfare as a primary target for groups opposed to government entitlements.

Certainly, understanding the laws behind the Medicaid program is crucial and the logical place to start, but fashioning an effective strategy to defend or promote specific programmatic interests requires a far more sophisticated understanding of the multiple potential pressure points that can lead to change.

Define the Problem

The first step in solving your Medicaid problem is to develop a clear understanding of the issue you are trying to resolve. This may be obvious — for example, where a specific service is not covered under the program or where rates paid under the program are inadequate. But often, it is not.

Start with the operational problem, which only you know best, and be clear about what the problem is and what it is not. It is the norm for an organization that derives a substantial percentage of its revenue from the

Medicaid program to have a long list of complaints, from petty to dire, about the program's implementation. Not all of these are worthy of your time or regulators' attention. Parse out your priorities and let the rest go. Resist the temptation to pile on — you will damage your credibility with regulators and undermine the clarity of your case. Finally, look for ways that your own internal business practices may be contributing to the problem, and own what is yours. If you complain that the program is failing to reimburse for a covered service, are you sure you are complying with proper claims procedures? Rest assured that regulators, who are loath to change program operations or policy, will be looking for ways to put the ball back in your court.

Once the problem has been clearly identified, it is important to trace it to its source. Medicaid is governed by a web of state and federal statutes, regulations, and administrative directives, as well as entrenched administrative practices that can impact the program's practical implementation as much as law. Determining the source of the problem will help clarify the available strategies for a solution, whether litigation, administrative advocacy, or legislative change.

Develop and Effectuate a Strategy to Address the Problem

As a starting point, it is always important to question whether the practice or policy in question is prohibited by law. Federal and state Medicaid statutes offer protections, including various procedural rights, which can be overlooked in implementation. State agencies are generally eager to avoid costly litigation, and where there is a clear statutory claim, they will often take administrative action to remedy the situation. Where existing law offers or even arguably offers a solution to a problem plaguing your operations, it makes sense to approach the state Medicaid agency.

Regardless of whether the goal is to change practice, policy, or law, a multi-faceted strategy is often the best path to achieving change in the Medicaid program. Being right — or having the better argument — is not always enough to persuade regulators to reverse a practice that has been in place for years or to initiate practices for the first time. Therefore, to the maximum extent possible, be prepared to show how your interpretation of the law, and the action you are requesting, advances sound public policy.

Our approach can be organized under four P's: policy, politics, potential allies, and pressure points.

- *Policy*

Policy refers to the process of building a practical case for the change that is sought. How will the change impact the larger program and the various constituencies Medicaid serves? What are the consequences of staying with the status quo? It is important not only to understand the answers to these questions, but also to harness data and anecdotes that can provide vivid illustrations of the problem, and help bring credibility to proposed solutions.

- *Politics*

Because Medicaid is a government program that consumes substantial portions of state and federal budgets — and in some states, local budgets — it is susceptible to intense political pressure and scrutiny. Ultimately, most policymakers want to be able to defend their actions as contributing to the quality and/or integrity of the program. Increasingly, political leaders are under intense pressure to contain program costs. Identify the potential political implications of your goals — what constituencies will be affected and at what cost. Craft your arguments in ways that are most likely to be heard within the current political environment.

- *Potential Allies*

State Medicaid programs have a host of sometimes competing constituencies: consumers (themselves often divided by population or health condition), providers, health plans, pharmaceutical companies, professional trade organizations, labor unions, and many others. Developing a strategic understanding of the various stakeholder groups and their interests will help build a base of support for — or neutralize opposition to — your cause.

- *Pressure Points*

Having assembled a compelling case and base of support from key allies, it is time to reach out to key decision-makers. Frequently, a handful of people in a state serve as gatekeepers to a state's Medicaid program. Understand who those people are, what authority or influence they have in the process, and how to access them to make your case. Ideally, these relationships should be cultivated over time, and not just at the moments when you need something or have a complaint.

Case Studies

The following case studies show how the strategies discussed above can come together to influence programmatic implementation over time in ways that support the business interests of stakeholders in the Medicaid program.

Gaining Entry into the Medicaid Market

Entering the Medicaid market is fairly straightforward for traditional health care providers. But for a host of businesses offering a range of products and services that are not directly reimbursable under the program, the path of entry requires a more strategic approach.

One client, a startup technology company, had developed an innovative clinical decision support product and sought to create an opportunity for the product to be piloted within the Medicaid program. State regulators had exhibited an interest in disease management as a vehicle to contain costs and improve care, but most of the initiatives under consideration were provider-focused and did not contemplate the capabilities of the company's product. The client tapped into that interest, providing extensive educational briefings and data showing their technology-based product's success in controlling costs and improving care quality. At the same time, through one-on-one briefings, the company cultivated relationships with key elected officials that had influence over the state's Medicaid program. Multiple stakeholder groups had been urging passage of legislation to test disease management within the Medicaid program. The client joined this effort and ensured that key elected officials were educated about their product's track record of success in other states and in the commercial market. The client also drafted model legislation for a disease management demonstration program that included technology-based solutions. Ultimately, legislation was passed — with the full support of state regulators — that authorized the creation of a disease management demonstration program and, reflecting the client's model language, specifically identified technology-based decision support as one of the desired approaches.

Seeking an Increase in Provider Rates

The rates paid to providers under Medicaid are set by the states through processes that often are more likely to reflect state budgetary pressures than market forces, such as medical inflation. As a result, it is not uncommon for providers to claim that the rates they are paid under Medicaid are inadequate, and efforts to increase rates are often particularly challenging.

When inadequate reimbursement rates put a home care agency's home nursing program for children in jeopardy, the client sought our assistance in setting their claim apart from the chorus of rate-related complaints. It quickly became apparent that the agency had a diverse base of potential allies in their cause. Meetings with hospital social work and financial departments revealed that children, unable to find nurses to care for them at home, were routinely staying in hospital beds far longer than necessary. This placed a significant financial burden on hospitals, which are paid per admission, not per day. Intermediate care facilities, too, were experiencing a backlog due to their inability to discharge children when medically appropriate. And, of course, the greatest impact was on the beneficiaries — children who were unable to be reunited with their families and were being cared for in conditions that research had demonstrated did not meet their developmental or health care needs.

The home care agency formed a coalition of the various stakeholders, including advocates for children and families, to develop a solution. The coalition conducted research to document the problem, gathered personal testimony and photographs from effected families, and crafted a legislative advocacy agenda geared toward not only increasing the rates, but also including other changes aimed at improving access to home nursing services for children. Drawing upon an analysis of existing research and available data, the coalition was also able to illustrate that the changes they sought would likely be at least cost neutral, if not produce a cost savings, to the Medicaid program because of decreased reliance on institutional care.

Protecting and Expanding Market Share

One successful effort with which this firm has been involved for more than a decade concerns the fifteen health plans in New York State that are sponsored by hospitals, community health centers, and physicians (provider-sponsored plans). In the early 1990s, New York's governor announced his intention to seek federal approval to transform the state's Medicaid managed care program by requiring most Medicaid beneficiaries to enroll in a health plan. The then commissioner of health testified that she believed commercial health plans were the best partner for the state. This announcement spurred three of the six then licensed provider-sponsored plans in the state to organize a coalition of provider-sponsored health plans.

The first challenge the coalition faced was to demonstrate the value provider-sponsored plans brought to the Medicaid program. With foundation support, the coalition published and disseminated a report showing the role provider-sponsored plans played in supporting safety net health care providers — providers that depended on Medicaid volume and revenue. These plans could not be written off easily — at least not by policy makers concerned about the continuing viability of the health care safety net. With that document in hand, a year later, the coalition secured legislation requiring the state to assign a larger number of members to provider-sponsored health plans.

In the late 1990s, Medicaid premiums plummeted and every Medicaid plan in New York State began losing money. Working closely with commercial health plans, providers, unions, and consumers, the coalition began a campaign to persuade state regulators and the legislature to increase premiums. While there is often an uneasy relationship between health plans, consumers, and providers, we found common ground on the premise that inadequate premiums portended inadequate care for consumers and inadequate reimbursement for providers — results that were in no one's interest. Thus, diverse stakeholders came together around a common goal, even as they opposed each other on other issues. We focused on legislators,

29

regulators, Washington and Albany, and the media. Ultimately, plan premiums were increased, in part through administrative action and more substantially through state legislation. By the end of the 1990s, premium rates were covering health plan costs. However, by that time, most of the commercial plans that had other product lines had fled the Medicaid market.

The work of the past decade has paid off for provider-sponsored health plans. Twelve years after the commissioner of health thought them irrelevant and nine years after many were on the verge of financial collapse, they are central players in the state's Medicaid managed care program. Today, there are fifteen provider-sponsored plans throughout New York serving more than 1.7 million public insurance beneficiaries. The plans are financially sound and are providing financial support to their provider-sponsors. Ultimately, the provider-sponsored health plans were able to secure the laws, regulations, and rules they needed to operate successfully because of their multifaceted approach. They aligned themselves with other stakeholders, most especially beneficiaries and their advocates; they were in tune to the surrounding political environment; they paid attention to the policy priorities inherent in their business, namely providing high-quality, cost-effective care to low-income patient populations; and they developed an ongoing and successful working relationship with the regulators and other policymakers who held decision-making authority over the program.

Conclusion

While Medicaid can be a fickle, unreliable, frustrating, and often seemingly irrational partner, there is no denying its clout in the marketplace. Changes in policy, practice, or law can shift millions of dollars, advancing public health goals and making or breaking a business. Medicaid can underwrite capital expansions, facilitate new product penetration, and promote advancements in clinical practices. However, Medicaid is first and foremost an insurance program for our nation's most vulnerable health care consumers. When approached with an understanding of how the program works, a commitment to the program's mission, and an effective strategy to ensure that your business interests are met, the risks of participating in state Medicaid programs can be managed, and your efforts met with considerable success.

Ms. Deborah Bachrach *is co-chair of her firm's nonprofit practice group, having previously co-chaired the firm's health industry practice group. She provides legislative, regulatory, and strategic counsel to a range of health care organizations and businesses that include hospitals, community health centers, health plans, mental health and substance abuse facilities, and long-term care agencies.*

Ms. Bachrach counsels health care providers and plans on revenue enhancement strategies with a special focus on government insurance programs. She has developed and secured passage of legislation providing additional operating and capital support for Medicaid-dependent hospitals, community health centers, and health plans. Ms. Bachrach has also assisted clients in obtaining state and federal licenses, contracts, and approvals, and developing viable organizational structures. Ms. Bachrach is a frequent speaker on public health insurance programs, and has published numerous articles and foundation-supported analyses of the effectiveness of these programs.

Between 1987 and 1992, Ms. Bachrach served as vice president of external affairs at St. Luke's-Roosevelt Hospital Center. Before joining St. Luke's-Roosevelt, she served as chief assistant attorney general in the office of the New York state attorney general. She graduated with honors from the New York University School of Law and the Wharton School of the University of Pennsylvania.

Ms. Melinda Dutton *provides strategic, regulatory, and government relations counsel to health and human services organizations and health care businesses. Her expertise focuses on public health insurance programs, including Medicaid, SCHIP, and Medicare, and health information technology. Prior to joining Manatt, she served for nine years at the Children's Defense Fund in New York, where she helped to develop and secure passage of legislation expanding publicly funded health insurance programs for children. Ms Dutton has published numerous reports and crafted multiple public campaigns to influence public policies related to the health and wellbeing of low-income children and families.*

Ms. Dutton graduated with honors from Columbia Law School. She is admitted to practice in the state of New York.

Avoiding Legal Pitfalls
in the Pharmaceutical Industry

Alan E. Schabes
Partner
Benesch, Friedlander, Coplan & Aronoff LLP

Helping Clients Develop a Strategy

Before you discuss developing legal strategy with respect to the pharmaceutical industry, you first have to divide the pharmaceutical industry into a number of different segments. You have the manufacturers, the wholesalers, and the retail outlets, and then you have the institutional area. Each of these realms has similar but different considerations. For example, on the manufacturer's side, there are a number of issues that are particular to them. Issues related to clinical tests, FDA approval, and intellectual property in terms of patenting individual drugs are some examples of the manufacturer's separate concerns. They don't necessarily apply to any of the other entities down the chain.

There are other issues that apply to the wholesalers, retailers, and institutional pharmacy sellers, and they are primarily related to pricing, marketing, fraud, and abuse. Those have been the primary issues the regulators are concerned with in terms of the downstream entities. When I help my clients develop a legal strategy, what I try to do is use that framework of issues. I sit down with them to decide what their issues are now and what they have been in the past. We use that as a mental checklist in order to go through the issues the client is concerned about.

I try to understand their business. For example, if we are dealing with a manufacturer, understanding their business is all about knowing how they get their product, how they do their research and development, and how they develop their product through the research and development phase, the testing phase, the clinical trial phase, and ultimately through the FDA approval. It is about how they market the product through their relationship with the wholesalers. The manufacturer's relationships are also important in terms of patenting and obtaining the necessary patents for intellectual property protection on both domestic and international levels.

Once we get moving downstream, I deal with wholesalers. In that relationship, it is central to understand how they buy the product, how they sell the product, how they market the product, and what kind of pricing they use. I need to know how they control access to the product and deal with generics. Understanding their business is critical in order for me to help them as best as I can. This understanding applies to the retail side of things as well as the institutional pharmacy side, which are the entities dispensing primarily to either nursing homes or hospitals.

Between the client and myself, the only way to resolve problems is to understand the business reasons behind what they want to do. I try to bring together and connect the legal realities and legal requirements with the business purpose. If you achieve a legally satisfactory result that does not achieve the business result, then you haven't done anything significant for your client. Of course, if you have achieved a business result that is not consistent with a legal result, then likewise, you have done nothing. Matching the two is absolutely critical. As far as a regulator or another party is concerned, I am a big believer in trying to resolve matters short of litigation and the potentially resulting hostility. You can always get into hostilities later, and you can always get into litigation.

Litigation resolves almost nothing. In some instances, it is inevitable, but clients are rarely happy in the midst of litigation or afterward. If they win litigation, it is usually after a great deal of expense, and those costs are usually much more than anyone anticipated. If they lose the litigation, then of course it is even worse, and you enter into a series of appeals. As far as litigation is concerned, the American system rarely resolves anything quickly or in a cost-efficient manner. Consequently, I am particularly in favor of resolving matters through mediation. If you must go to litigation, then my experience is that arbitration in front of an informed and experienced panel of arbitrators is much more favorable than going to court.

Common Legal Issues for Pharmaceutical Companies

As far as manufacturers go, their most common legal issues are likely to involve clinical trials and getting them approved with institutional review boards. Manufacturers frequently run into legal problems in matters of FDA approval, intellectual property protection, pricing in relation to downstream distributors like manufacturers and retailers, and fraud and abuse. As far as wholesalers, retailers, and institutional pharmacies are concerned, one of the main issues is fraud and abuse as it relates to the federal and state anti-kickback statutes. The federal anti-kickback statute says that one cannot pay for or receive anything of value in order to induce the purchase of an object or item that is reimbursable under Medicare or

Medicaid. That is a big issue. Other retailer issues may be anti-trust as it relates to pricing and access, contracts with manufacturers and pharmaceutical benefit managers, contracts with suppliers, and contracts with other distribution outlets further downstream.

In order for us to help with each of these issues, we need to have an understanding of their particular business goals and the business results they want to achieve. Trying to bring their business result together with the legal reality, and trying to carve creative but legally safe solutions, are our main objectives when helping them to reach their goals.

Steering Clear of Potential Problems

When manufacturers are dealing with, for example, clinical trials and relationships with institutional review boards, the main step toward avoiding potential legal issues is understanding the integrity of their own research. The pharmaceutical company needs to know how the institutional review board system works, and how to get those approvals done. It is essential to know what is acceptable and what is not. In relationship to intellectual property protection, it is key to understand what is patentable and what is not. The company must know the process for getting a domestic or international patent, and understand what the patent will protect and what it will not. Understanding the fraud and abuse rules, the anti-kickback rules, and government regulators' attitudes with respect to rebates is absolutely critical.

When it comes to fraud and abuse issues, having all of that knowledge goes very far for a lawyer trying to protect a manufacturer. Downstream with the wholesalers, retailers, and institutional pharmacies, again, the central concern is having them understand the legal realities. Know the fraud and abuse issues, the anti-trust issues, and anything else that will come up over and over again as they deal with the manufacturer. Can you take rebates or not? When dealing with a retailer, find out what you can give a retailer in order to have them buy from you. Be aware of the kinds of inducements you can offer. If there are certain inducements you cannot offer, know how you will deal with that. Understanding the legal realities allows for a melding of business strategies in a legally defensible and protected way.

The rules involving the FDA and FDA approval are huge for the manufacturer. Laws relating to protection of intellectual property are also significant. Fraud and abuse rules and anti-kickbacks are critical concerns for downstream distributors. Knowing what you can and cannot do is vital. Any federal and state approvals one needs in order to engage in their activities are laws you need to be concerned about. Always know basic contractual law as it relates to dealing with both upstream and downstream participants in the process.

The Time for Litigation

Litigation becomes necessary when you cannot resolve the matter through mediation or negotiation. The types of cases that usually end up in court are the ones that involve the protection of an intellectual property, because you need an absolute yes or no answer. That kind of thing is not usually negotiable. Contractual relationships may be more resolvable through negotiation. An issue of reaching or not reaching a given profit margin can sometimes be resolved with a compromise. When you are dealing with the absolute ownership of a patent or rights, the answer is absolute, and those cases typically go to litigation.

From an intellectual property standpoint, in order to prosecute another company for a client, you need to understand the patent your client has developed and the intellectual property aspects of it. You must understand the competing intellectual property of the other client, and once you know all of that, you can then file an action against the party that is allegedly infringing upon your intellectual property. If you were seeking to protect your own intellectual property, then you would invoke the protection of the federal court by establishing your right to your own intellectual property. If, on the other hand, you were defending your right to use an item of intellectual property, then obviously it would be a different set of circumstances.

If I were defending my client, I would have to understand what the client did or did not do. I would have to know whether they infringed on the patent. You must understand the original patent and the original intellectual property protection the plaintiff had, and you must know whether your client infringed upon it. This leads you to an awareness of whether you have a legitimate defense or not. That is critical. Often, it is not a black and white issue, although we would like it to be. But knowing what you have is critical to your ability to defend a case. You get into trouble with clients when you do not give them an appropriate judgment of how strong or weak you believe their case to be. They move ahead to litigation and end up unhappy, because you never gave them an accurate assessment up front. In order to defend a client, you must really understand the strengths and weaknesses of their case.

Routine Misconceptions about the Pharmaceutical Industry

There are several misconceptions about the laws or legal issues affecting pharmaceutical companies. The first of these would be the idea that it is easy and inexpensive to obtain FDA approval of a product. The belief that pharmaceutical companies try to cut corners in clinical trials and try to rush their product to market is mistaken. It is very, very unusual for any corners to be cut or for there to be any kind of curtailment of the process. That is a big misconception. There are misunderstandings about the litigation involving the drugs the FDA ultimately pulls off the market. It is very rarely the case that a drug pulled off the market has not had any kind of warnings associated with it before. That is what usually creates the liability.

For example, in the Vioxx case we are witnessing now, the Cleveland Clinic issued articles many years ago questioning the side effects of Vioxx. The question was whether Merck paid attention to unfavorable research results, took that into account, and dealt with it as they were marketing Vioxx. But the gross misconception is that a manufacturer can rush to market with a particular drug without doing the necessary clinical trial and getting the necessary FDA approval, or that they are somehow able buy their way through that process. I have never found that to be the case.

Words of Wisdom

The best piece of business advice I have ever received is to really understand the business reason for what a pharmaceutical company has done. The business justification is the predicate. I have yet to meet a pharmaceutical company that acts in a blatantly irresponsible manner. There is always some sort of business justification for whatever they do, whether it is right, wrong, or somewhere in the middle. The best legal business advice I have heard is to understand that business reason thoroughly, then remember that in the context of the legal advice you are giving. Keep it in your mind so you always understand where they're coming from. There are very few black and white situations. There are very few situations where one side is right and one is wrong. Ultimately, there is almost always a legitimate and understandable business rationale for what has been done.

Avoiding Legal Issues

Reducing Exposure to Legal Risks

If I were to discuss minimizing legal issues with any C-level executive from a pharmaceutical company, my approach would consist of a number of fundamental questions. When it comes to manufacturers, they have to understand their products and how that product will be developed. A manufacturer has to understand the intellectual property protection they have or can get. It is essential to know how the company arrived at that product, meaning how it was developed from a research and development standpoint. They must know if there were any infringements that took place before it was taken to market. How did it go through the clinical trial process? How agreements were constructed with the institutional review boards, and were the trials done appropriately and with reputable researchers? You have to be able to verify that the results were reported reliably, or if there were any oversights in terms of the results. When the decision was made to move forward, were both good and bad results taken into account with equal measure? I would ask if they understood any and all of the FDA's concerns as they went through the approval process. Did they take every step they needed to take? At that point, once they had FDA approval, how did they construct a relationship with downstream distributors? I would advise the executive to know what kinds of rebates they are providing, and if those rebates are justified from a legitimate business standpoint. It is important that they consider any concerns the federal government may have had with respect to rebates and pricing, and that they are pricing it appropriately.

With respect to wholesalers, my conversation would be about how they buy their product. I would want to know what kind of relationship they have with the manufacturers. I would ask what kinds of rebates they are giving and what kinds they are pushing down. I would be interested in how they sell to their retailers and what kinds of inducements they give them. The wholesaler executive needs to know how they protect the supply line and, ultimately, the relationship with the purchasers. They should recognize exactly what kind of relationships they have with their manufacturers. From an anti-trust standpoint, they should be aware of any issues. Again, from a fraud and abuse standpoint, understand what is there, what the requirements are, and what to avoid.

Legal Landmines with Financial Impact

As mentioned earlier, for manufacturers, the greatest legal landmines a pharmaceutical company can encounter are in the areas of clinical trials, the FDA, and fraud and abuse. For wholesalers, they would be fraud and abuse, the relationship with their manufacturers, and the relationship with downstream distributors. Retailers and institutional pharmacies may stumble upon legal landmines in the relationship with upstream suppliers, in the area of fraud and abuse, or simply with state and federal regulation of their activity.

Each of these entities has to have a compliance department, which has been suggested by the United States Department of Health and Human Services Office of Inspector General. This department has come up with a work plan for the pharmaceutical industry, and the plan is something that will be a guideline in terms of compliance. Every kind of company that is involved in this industry has to have an active and operating compliance function, and a senior executive must be in charge of compliance and reliably report to the board of directors. This system is absolutely critical in order to find the issues before regulators find them.

Keeping an Eye on the Law

Laws relating to FDA approval are constantly changing. The laws related to fraud and abuse, which the Office of Inspector General and other regulators look at, are also constantly being tweaked. Licensure laws and certification laws related to payors are, again, constantly being reviewed.

The most significant recent development from a reimbursement standpoint is the enactment of the new Medicare prescription drug law. It is a new benefit called Medicare Part D, and it is huge because it creates a new payor source for pharmaceuticals and a new system for selling drugs to the elderly. As a distributor, and even as a manufacturer, that is something you will have to understand and take appreciation of. That benefit will clearly be a major source of pharmaceutical revenue in the future. In situations like this, you have to understand the program and how the program works.

Potential Marketing Pitfalls

Some actions, specifically those taken in the marketing area, can get the pharmaceutical company into legal trouble. One example of this would be giving illegal inducements that violate the fraud and abuse laws. The federal anti-kickback law states that one cannot pay or receive anything of value in order to induce the purchase of an item that is reimbursable under Medicare and Medicaid. Most drugs are reimbursable under Medicaid. After the Medicare plan goes into effect, the majority of drugs will be reimbursable under Medicare. Most marketers are used to giving something of value in order to induce somebody to buy, whether it is a rebate, a discount, or perhaps something as innocuous as giving something of value for a referral. Methods that are completely understandable and legitimate in the automobile industry are a felony in the pharmaceutical industry when you are dealing with Medicare and Medicaid.

The unsophisticated, or those who are newcomers to the industry, have difficulty understanding this. They might think to themselves that a particular marketing idea has worked well in the automobile industry or in some other kind of distribution company, but in the context of the pharmaceutical industry, it is completely illegal. Once that is understood, you are fine. People will certainly still try to push the envelope, but they should understand that doing so could easily get a company into big trouble.

A Different Industry with Different Legal Issues

Legal landmines in the pharmaceutical industry are unique because of the patchwork of federal and state regulation. The pharmaceutical industry is one of the most highly regulated industries, and the regulations apply to manufacturing, federal approval to bring it to market, and distribution. Every single step of bringing a drug to market and distributing that drug is regulated in some federal or state aspect.

There is also a unique aspect in the complexity of a pharmaceutical case. The characteristic of intellectual property is certainly unique. Other than that, a pharmaceutical case is similar to other kinds of health care cases. If you are not familiar with health care and the patchwork of regulation that comes with the territory, then the pharmaceutical industry will seem very foreign. If, however, you are familiar with general health care and with the issues of health care clients, then the pharmaceutical realm is pretty much the same. The exceptions are the intellectual property, the FDA approval, and the regulations during the manufacturing process.

The settlements in these cases are distinctive because of their sheer scope and magnitude. We are talking about huge amounts of money, and the complexity of the settlements is mind-boggling. Witness this by looking at all of the recent settlements we have seen. Dow-Corning went into Chapter 11 attempting to resolve the issue of their silicone breast implants. Fen-Phen litigation made headlines, and there have been numerous other large drug settlements. We see the most obvious differences between this and other litigation with recalls, which have involved the appointment of a special master, a consolidation of the cases, and numerous class actions that are filed. Resolving that number of cases, each with such a large scale, are litigation and settlement processes that are very specific to pharmaceuticals.

Steps to Avoid Legal Issues

1. Understand the regulations that apply to you. The pharmaceutical industry is one of the most highly regulated industries. There are reams of statutes and regulations that apply to almost every aspect of the industry. If there is not a thorough understanding of the regulatory scheme, legal problems are inevitable.
2. Before you take a product to market, pay close attention to any bad news you find and take it into account. Bad news will never remain a secret. Although the decision to discontinue the development of a product after a significant amount of research and development has

been done is costly, the costs are small compared to those that are incurred in connection with recalling a product that has been on the market.

3. Do not market by using inducements, unless legal counsel has reviewed them carefully.

4. Be careful about pricing in terms of how you price the product; it can often get you into trouble. No pharmaceutical company can afford a conviction for violating a fraud and abuse law. Indeed, there isn't a pharmaceutical company whose business can withstand a publicly announced investigation. Improper inducements and pricing policies can easily result in investigations and, ultimately, charges of wrongdoing.

5. Be very careful about the relationships you have with your downstream distributors, and make sure that relationship not only complies with applicable federal and state regulations, but that it also makes sense from a commercial standpoint.

Mr. Alan E. Schabes is a partner with his firm's health care practice group and serves as a member of the firm's executive committee. He focuses his practice on health care law, including the presentation of long-term care and residential care facilities, physician groups, integrated delivery systems, ancillary service providers, including institutional pharmacy companies, health maintenance organizations, preferred provider organizations, Medicare and Medicaid reimbursement matters, fraud and abuse, asset and stock acquisitions, and joint venture formation.

Mr. Schabes currently serves as the vice chair of the "Long Term Care and the Law" program for the American Health Lawyers Association. Mr. Schabes served as the co-general editor of The Long-Term Care Handbook, *published in 2000 by the American Health Lawyers Association. Mr. Schabes has been credentialed by the American Medical Association to serve as a member of the AMA Doctor Advisory Network. He was named the recipient of the 1992 Journalism Award of the Ohio chapter of the American College of Health care Administrators.*

Mr. Schabes has spoken nationally on a variety of health care topics to groups including the American Health Lawyers Association, the American College of Health Care Administrators, the American Association of Homes for the Aging, and the Ohio Health care Association.

He received his B.S., magna cum laude, from Duquesne University in 1978. Mr. Schabes earned his J.D. in 1981 from Hofstra University, where he served as associate editor of the Hofstra University Law Review.

Legal Strategies for Health Care Providers

Howard Bogard

Partner

Burr & Forman LLP

Over the past year, the news has been filled with stories of health care providers, both big and small, who have committed improper acts—a hospital bills Medicare for services not provided, a physician uses a billing code that results in greater reimbursement even though a different code is more appropriate (a tactic called "up coding"), or a therapist pays for patient referrals. It is easy to see why such conduct is illegal. But do not be fooled—the business of health care is like no other. Common business practices may very well be improper when health care providers are involved. Further, the laws affecting the health care industry are numerous, complicated, and often unfamiliar to many providers.

Take, for example, a software salesman who, in an attempt to sell his products to a small business, invites several of the owners and their spouses out to an expensive dinner. He also provides free tickets to a football game and promises to "throw in" software. To close the deal the salesman informs the group that they will be eligible for a "referral fee" if they help the salesman meet other prospective customers. A normal business practice? In many industries, the answer is "yes" and such practice is entirely appropriate. But now consider a similar scenario involving a physician practice and a salesman for a durable medical equipment supplier. Any concerns with the salesman using the same approach? Absolutely. Any actions intended to induce patient referrals or the purchase of health care products or services can violate both civil and criminal laws, subjecting health care providers to hefty monetary penalties, exclusion from federal health care programs, and even prison terms.

It has been said that the business of health care is the most regulated industry in the United States, second only to the nuclear energy industry. Illustrating this point, a recent publication of federal laws affecting health care providers is over 2,000 pages (in very small type). Add state laws, Medicare and Medicaid reimbursement manuals, third-party payor requirements, advisory opinions, fraud alerts, and compliance program guidance and it becomes even more apparent why it is so challenging for health care providers to remain compliant.

Aside from the sheer volume of laws affecting health care providers, regulatory compliance can be complicated for several other reasons. First, many health care laws are not clearly stated or narrowly defined. Take, for example, the federal anti-kickback statute, which makes it a criminal offense for anyone to knowingly and willfully solicit, receive, offer, or pay anything of value to induce or reward the referral of business covered by a federal health care program, including Medicare or Medicaid. Sounds fairly straight forward, but in reality the law is so broadly drafted that since 1991 the Department of Health and Human Services ("HHS") has published 22 "Safe Harbors," which exempt from prosecution common health care arrangements that otherwise might violate the anti-kickback statute. The Office of Inspector General ("OIG") has issued over 100 formal advisory opinions, most of which help to clarify the scope and application of the anti-kickback statute. Not surprisingly, anti-kickback statute issues are often hard to detect and eliminate.

A second barrier to regulatory compliance is that many health care laws are not well known. Take, for example, a federal law that makes it illegal for a physician to place an ad in the newspaper that reads: "Dr. Smith is a cardiologist approved by both the Medicare and Medicaid programs." By law, it is unlawful for a health care provider to create the false impression that he or she is endorsed by Medicare or Medicaid. Examples of other arrangements that many providers are surprised to learn can be problematic include: providing free transportation to a patient; referring a Medicare patient to a clinical lab that is owned, even in part, by the spouse of the physician's grandparent or grandchild; waiving co-payments, except for specific and documented hardship cases; failing to conduct a background check that would reveal that an employed health care provider is excluded from participation in a federal health care program.

Finally, even when the government tries to calm the fears of the provider community regarding the broad scope of the health care laws, the results can often be less than reassuring. In October 2000, the OIG released a statement indicating that physicians and other providers will not be subject to criminal, civil, or administrative penalties for innocent billing errors or even negligence. Rather, under the federal False Claims Act only offenses that are committed with actual knowledge, reckless disregard, or deliberate ignorance of the falsity of the claim will be pursued. The problem, however, is that in many cases there is a fine line between an "innocent" (or even negligent) billing mistake and acting with "reckless disregard" or "deliberate ignorance." For example, a provider assigns certain billing functions to an untrained office member without inquiring whether the employee has the requisite knowledge and training to accurately file such claims. An innocent or negligent action? According to the OIG, the provider could be found to have acted with reckless disregard and as a result could face civil penalties under the False Claims Act.

The First Step

How does an attorney help a provider address all of the various health care legal requirements? A good first step is to develop a legal/compliance strategy. To do so, an attorney must first develop a complete and substantive understanding of the provider's business. Not only is it important to comprehend the specific services the provider offers and in what capacity (e.g., inpatient or outpatient; surgical, diagnostic, or therapeutic; for-profit or non-profit), but also to learn about the provider's one, three, and five-year business plan, what markets it wants to expand into, what markets it wants to leave, and what new products/services it wants to offer.

To obtain an understanding that is more than superficial, an attorney must meet with the key people working in the provider's business. It is important to learn their concerns, both legal and operational. Have there been any government investigations, any significant lawsuits, are there any issues or concerns that affect that person's job responsibilities? The question can be posed as simply as: "What are the major concerns about the business?" While this question may only elicit an answer concerning financial and operational concerns, within those responses will be legal "issues" that the attorney can use to assist the provider in meeting specific business goals, or the attorney can identify as potential impediments.

Developing a Compliance Strategy

Based on the attorney's understanding of a provider's business, and working with upper level management, a general, legal strategy can be developed. I am a firm believer that a lawyer's role is to help a client obtain their business objectives as efficiently as possible and in compliance with applicable laws. A word of caution, however. Each provider, even if operating within the same market and providing the same services, will have different legal needs and objectives. Consequently, it is important to develop a unique legal strategy. A generic approach will not work in the long term and the provider (the client) will feel as if its needs are not being met. It is important to become a partner with the provider, not in the legal sense but in the operational sense. If an attorney takes the time to get to know the provider's business and becomes invested personally in the provider's successes and legal issues, the provider will be satisfied.

The legal strategies that I utilize are situational to a great extent and are client focused. For example, if fraud and abuse or regulatory compliance is a key issue, then I will formulate a compliance approach based on requirements under state and federal anti-kickback and Stark Laws, as well as other fraud and abuse regulations. Within that context, there are strategies a provider can take to automate the compliance process. For example, the provider (with the help of an attorney well versed in health care regulatory issues) can develop form agreements to cover various topics such as physician employment and recruitment, medical director agreements, and service provider agreements. Standardized forms and processes not only help to eliminate regulatory compliance issues, but also save money. By establishing baseline parameters and a formal review process, compliance errors brought about by the normal negotiation process can be eliminated.

Compliance Issues

If a legal issue is identified, it is important for the attorney to sit down face-to-face with key people in the organization, obtain their views, and then review any of the applicable documents. For example, if the issue involves a contract, it is important to review not only the contract, but also related material, such as correspondence, e-mails, and even rough drafts. If the issue concerns a billing matter, it might be appropriate to ask the provider to perform some type of internal billing audit to determine the scope and extent of the problem. Steps should be taken, however, to conduct any audit, to the extent possible, at the direction of an attorney so as to obtain the protections of the attorney-client privilege. It goes without saying that the attorney will also need to look at the various laws that apply to the issue under review. Based on interviews and the examination of applicable documents and legal requirements, the attorney should devise a strategy to deal with the issue.

Regardless of the legal matter, it is important that an attorney tailor the strategy to the situation and balance legal compliance with business issues. Sometimes they work well together and sometimes they do not. However, an attorney's job is to advise the client of the legal issues, present them with options, and then the provider makes a decision based on the information. I often use a risk/benefit curve to describe the options.

The greater the benefit to the provider, more often the greater the risk, and conversely the same is true. Obviously, the attorney must clearly point out any options that are illegal or which carry a significant legal risk. However, many times problems have multiple solutions and varying degrees of risk. It is up to the provider to determine which "legal" option to pursue after weighing all of the facts and circumstances. With the right information, the provider can make a well-informed business decision.

Common Legal Issues for Health Care Companies

As stated above, there are literally hundreds of laws affecting health care providers in the United States, along with a myriad of government agencies tasked with enforcement, including the Office of Inspector General, the Internal Revenue Service, the Department of Justice, the United States Attorney General, various State Attorneys General, and the Federal Trade Commission. Specifically, laws related to fraud and abuse, which generally include the anti-kickback statute, the Stark Laws, and the False Claims Act, along with the privacy and security regulations published pursuant to the Health Insurance Portability and Accountability Act of 1996 ("HIPAA"), generally affect all health care providers, including physicians, hospitals, surgery centers, diagnostic centers, home health agencies, nursing homes, physical therapy providers, etc. Also of key importance are obligations for hospitals and physicians under the Emergency Medical Treatment and Active Labor Act ("EMTALA") and corporate responsibility issues for all providers.

The anti-kickback statute. The federal anti-kickback statute, 42 U.S.C. § 1320a-7b(b), prohibits, among other things, the offer, payment, solicitation, or acceptance of remuneration directly or indirectly in return for referring an individual to a provider of services for which payment may be made in whole or in part under a federal health care program, including the Medicare or Medicaid programs. Violation of the anti-kickback statute is a crime and is punishable by a fine of up to $50,000, five years imprisonment, and/or exclusion from participation in any federal health care programs, including the Medicare and Medicaid programs. For instance, a hospital cannot give a financial incentive to a physician to encourage the physician to send Medicare patients to the hospital. This incentive could be in the form of a direct payment, but often more subtle arrangements are involved, such as below fair market value lease agreements, free or discounted supplies, or payment to the physician for unjustified or unnecessary services.

Since the anti-kickback statute is a criminal statute, the government must establish that the defendant acted with the requisite knowledge (i.e., knowingly and willfully). Most federal courts that have considered the knowledge standard under the anti-kickback statute have adopted the "any purpose" or Greber test, which would find the requisite knowledge if one purpose, not necessarily the primary or sole purpose, of the remuneration is to induce referrals.

The Office of Inspector General ("OIG") of the Department of Health and Human Services ("HHS") has issued "Safe Harbor Regulations," which describe practices that will not be considered violations of the anti-kickback statute. The fact that a particular arrangement does not fall within a Safe Harbor does not mean that the arrangement violates the anti-kickback statute. Rather, the Safe Harbor Regulations simply provide a guarantee that qualifying arrangements do not violate the law. Thus, arrangements that do not qualify for Safe Harbor protection are in largely the same positions as they were prior to the promulgation of these regulations, and they must be carefully evaluated in light of the provisions of the anti-kickback statute.

The Stark Law. As originally enacted, the Ethics in Patient Referrals Act of 1989 (the "Stark Law") (codified at 42 U.S.C. § 1395nn) restricted physician investment in, and referrals to, clinical laboratory services furnished after January 1, 1992 to Medicare patients. With the passage of the Budget

Reconciliation Act of 1993, which, in relevant part, went into effect on January 1, 1995, the list of services restricted under the amended Stark Law (referred to as the "Stark II Law") was expanded to cover all "designated health services," which includes clinical laboratory services; physical therapy services; occupational therapy services; speech-language pathology services; radiology services, including magnetic resonance imaging, computerized axial tomography scans, and ultrasound services; radiation therapy service and supplies; durable medical equipment and supplies; parenteral and enteral nutrients, equipment and supplies, prosthetics, orthotics, and prosthetic devices and supplies; home health services; outpatient prescription services; and inpatient and outpatient hospital services.

Unless otherwise excepted by the Stark Law, a physician may not make a referral to an entity with whom the physician or a member of his or her immediate family has a financial relationship, which includes both investment interests as well as compensation relationships, for the provision of a designated health service that may be paid, in whole or in part, by either the Medicare or Medicaid programs, and any entity that accepts such prohibited referrals is prohibited from billing any payor for such services. Sanctions for prohibited referrals include the denial of Medicare and Medicaid payment for the services, the imposition of civil monetary penalties of up to $15,000 for each prohibited referral, and exclusion from the Medicare and Medicaid programs.

It is important to note that while the anti-kickback statute and the Stark Law appear similar in scope and intent, and "except" similar arrangements under the Anti-Kickback Safe Harbors and Stark Law Exceptions, respectively, it is critical that a provider confirm compliance with both laws. Oftentimes, a provider will assume (incorrectly) that compliance with an Anti-Kickback Safe Harbor will result in compliance with a Stark Law Exception, or vice versa. And remember, an arrangement that implicates the anti-kickback statute does not have to comply with a Safe Harbor to proceed, while an arrangement that implicates the referral prohibitions under the Stark Law must satisfy an applicable Stark Law Exception to proceed. In summary, any type of arrangement between referral sources must be separately analyzed under both the anti-kickback statute and the Stark Law.

The False Claims Act. The federal False Claims Act gives the federal government or private litigants on behalf of the federal government, i.e., whistleblowers, an additional way to police false bills or requests for payment for health care services. Under the False Claims Act, the government may fine any person who knowingly submits or causes the submission of claims for payment to the federal government that are false or fraudulent, or which contain false or misleading information. Further, any person who knowingly makes or uses a false record or statement to avoid paying the federal government may be subject to fines under the False Claims Act. The federal government has widely used the False Claims Act to enforce alleged Medicare and other governmental program fraud in areas such as coding errors, billing for services not provided, billing for services at higher reimbursement rate than is allowed, and billing for medically unnecessary care. The penalty for violation of the False Claims Act ranges from $5,500 to $10,000 for each false claim plus three times the amount of damages resulting from each false claim. Because of the severity of the penalties under the False Claims Act, health care providers often find it necessary to settle allegations of violations under the False Claims Act (regardless of the merits of such allegations) rather than risk an adverse outcome in a court of law.

In addition to the False Claims Act, the federal government has other civil and criminal statutes, which may be utilized if the government suspects that a provider has submitted false claims. Many states also have similar false claims statutes that impose liability for the types of acts prohibited by the False Claims Act but perpetrated against the state. Further, the submission of false claims may result in termination of a provider's participation in federal health care programs, including Medicare. In addition, managing employees of a provider and persons who actively participate in the submission of false claims can be excluded from participation in any federal health care program.

HIPAA. The Health Insurance Portability and Accountability Act of 1996 ("HIPAA") authorized HHS to issue regulations designed to protect the privacy and security of protected health information. Such regulations have proceeded along two courses: (1) the development of standards to ensure the privacy of protected health information (the "Privacy Regulations"), and (2) the development of standards to ensure the security of electronic protected health information (the "Security Regulations"). The final Privacy Regulations were originally issued in December 2000; however, HHS subsequently published revised "final" regulations on August 14, 2002. Most health care providers were required to comply with the final Privacy Regulations by April 14, 2003. In addition, final Security Regulations were issued on February 20, 2003, with an effective date of compliance of April 21, 2005 for most providers.

In their current form, the HIPAA regulations contain very broad and complex provisions which increase patient control over medical records, severely limit the ways that health care providers can use and disclose protected health information, and could subject health care providers to significant financial penalties for violating such regulations. The HIPAA regulations significantly affect health care providers as well as those consultants or business associates of a provider who have access to or transmit protected health information. The final Privacy and Security Regulations require providers to adopt privacy policies, designate privacy and security officers, and provide patients with certain notices regarding the provider's privacy practices.

EMTALA. The Emergency Medical Treatment and Active Labor Act ("EMTALA") was enacted in 1986 as part of the Consolidated Omnibus Budget Reconciliation Act of 1995 ("COBRA").[1] Since EMTALA's enactment, much literature has been written on this subject, offering participating hospitals and other health care providers guidance on how to interpret and comply with the requirements of EMTALA.[2] Congress enacted EMTALA in response to concerns that hospitals were turning away or transferring patients who were in need of emergency medical care but were unable to pay for the emergency services. Initially, EMTALA was passed in order to stop hospitals from "dumping" patients who were unable to pay for medical treatment and came to be known as the "Anti-Dumping Act." Today, EMTALA is a standard of practice for hospitals that participate in the federal Medicare program and physicians who are responsible for examination, treatment, or transfer of patients in an emergency department.

---

[1] P.L. 99-272; 42 U.S.C. § 1395dd.
[2] The Centers for Medicare and Medicaid Services ("CMS"), formerly known as the Health Care Financing Administration ("HCFA"), have issued interpretative guidelines that provide instructions and policy interpretations on several key issues under EMTALA (hereinafter referred to as the "Interpretative Guidelines").

EMTALA contains several major requirements for hospitals who participate in the Medicare program, including: (1) an obligation to provide a medical screening examination to any person who comes to the Emergency Department of a hospital and requests an examination or treatment for a medical problem; (2) the requirement that if an emergency medical condition is found, to provide further medical examination and treatment to stabilize that medical condition; (3) the requirement to transfer that patient to another medical facility if the hospital is unable to stabilize the patient within its capacity and capability; (4) the requirement not to delay examinations and/or treatment in order to inquire about the patient's insurance or payment status; (5) to accept appropriate transfers of patients with emergency medical conditions if the hospital has the specialized capabilities not available at the transferring hospital and has the capacity to treat those patients; (6) if the patient refuses examination, treatment or transfer, to obtain or attempt to obtain written and informed refusal of examination, treatment, or appropriate transfer; and (7) not to take adverse action against a physician or qualified medical personnel who refuses to transfer a patient with an emergency medical condition, or against an employee who reports a violation of these requirements.[3]

EMTALA applies to hospitals that have an Emergency Department ("ED") by requiring that these hospitals provide an appropriate medical screening examination ("MSE") for individuals who come in requesting an examination or treatment for a medical condition. The term "hospital with an Emergency Department" is defined as a hospital that offers services for emergency conditions within its capability to do so, including rural primary care facilities and psychiatric hospitals providing care for psychiatric emergencies.[4]

EMTALA requires a hospital ED to provide an appropriate MSE to any individual coming onto its premises, in order to determine if an emergency condition or active labor is present. The MSE must be conducted within the capability of the hospital's ED. If an emergency medical condition is found, the hospital must supply either stabilization prior to transferring the patient or a written certification, signed by a physician, which appropriately describes the transfer as appropriate and meets certain other conditions.

[3] See 42 U.S.C. § 1395dd; 42 C.F.R. §§ 489.20 and 489.24; Interpretative Guidelines p. V-16.
[4] 42 C.F.R. § 489.24(b).

On August 29, 2003, the Centers for Medicare & Medicaid Services ("CMS") released final regulations revising the EMTALA requirements for hospitals and physicians. The regulations became effective on November 10, 2003, and attempt to clarify when and where the EMTALA requirements apply. The final regulations also address the following: what is a "dedicated emergency department"; individuals who present to locations on a hospital campus other than a dedicated emergency department; individuals who come to a dedicated emergency department for non-emergency services; outpatient services; individuals who present to an off-campus department of a hospital; inpatient admissions; individuals who are in a hospital-owned ambulance; and physicians' on-call obligations.

Corporate Responsibility. In the aftermath of Enron, and with the enactment of the Sarbanes-Oxley Act, corporate responsibility for health care providers has become a significant issue. Recently, the United States Department of Health and Human Services, Office of Inspector General, in conjunction with the American Health Lawyers Association, published two resource guides for general counsel, compliance officers, and boards of directors of health care organizations. The purpose of the publications is to assist these individuals in carrying out their responsibilities in the current health care environment. Board members have a duty to exercise the proper amount of care in their decision making, which includes a duty to act in good faith, with that level of care that an ordinarily prudent person would exercise in like circumstances, and in a manner they reasonably believe is in the best interest of the corporation. Likewise, general counsel and compliance officers must support the board in its oversight responsibilities by ensuring that the board receives accurate information and candid advice.

How to Prevent Future Legal Issues

To avoid legal issues, a provider needs to be proactive rather then reactive. If a provider is reacting to a problem then it may have reached the point where it cannot be dealt with internally. For example, under the False Claims Act the government has indicated that it recognizes that providers make billing mistakes and that it will not prosecute such health care providers for errors or mistakes; instead, the government will ask that the overpayments be returned. However, there is a gray line between a billing issue caused by an error and one that is actionable under the False Claims

Act based on deliberate ignorance or reckless disregard. If a provider is not proactive, a billing problem that could have been prevented and addressed as a simple error but instead goes on for six months, a year, eighteen months, stops looking like an error and more like reckless disregard or deliberate ignorance. Further, whenever a provider is reacting to an issue, it is spending time and resources in solving the problem. Unfortunately, for most providers faced with increasing time demands, problems are "discovered" not "prevented." It is much more efficient and much more effective to be proactive, but also much harder.

There are several different ways to be proactive in compliance efforts but, most importantly, it takes commitment from top-level management. The C-level Executives need to create a culture of compliance throughout the company that stresses that compliance is important and that the company will strive to do the right thing, not only from a business perspective but from a legal perspective. To assist with this task, it is helpful for an organization to appoint a compliance officer. Essentially, a compliance officer will develop compliance policies (often called a compliance plan), oversee and monitor the implementation of the compliance plan, conduct compliance training and education, coordinate audits and investigations, and serve as a resource to employees within the organization, as well as board members and management. Specific responsibilities of a compliance officer are detailed in the OIG's various Compliance Program Guidance documents[5].

Minimizing Exposure to Legal Issues in Health Care

When advising executives of health care companies how to effectively minimize their exposure to legal issues, one of the best items of advice is for them to assemble a team of top level individuals who are knowledgeable about the applicable legal issues affecting the business and to ask these individuals to create a list of their top five or ten business/legal concerns.

Once a general list of issues is assembled by the various C-level Executives, the next task is to prioritize the list, with the number one item identified as presenting the most risk or greatest challenge to the organization. Once

---

[5] OIG Fraud Prevention & Detention Compliance Guidance, available at
http://www.oig.hhs.gov/fraud/complianceguidance.html

your list is complete, a provider should work from the top down, minimizing first its greatest risk area as much as possible. While the development of a compliance list may seem fairly simplistic, the complexity arises in the development of strategies and solutions to address the concerns.

Legal Landmines

There are quite a few legal landmines for health care companies. Any time a company is investigated by the government, whether it is because of a whistle-blower, an anonymous complaint or a lawsuit, it requires that an incredible amount of time, energy, and resources be pulled away from the business to address the investigation. I have been involved in numerous government investigations involving single physicians and small, rural facilities. While I believe the government is more likely to devote resources to larger cases that have a patient care significance, or that will serve to send a message about a widespread problem, it would be a mistake to think that a government investigation is limited to large companies.

When dealing with a government investigation, there are several important steps to take. First, a provider should retain experienced legal counsel immediately, and if there are accounting issues, a qualified accounting firm. Second, the attorney should immediately gather and review all of the relevant information in order to gain a complete understanding of the problem. Third, the attorney should interview the provider's employees that may have information relevant to the issue. Four, the attorney should identify the legal and business risks presented by the issues under investigation. Finally, it is important to begin a dialogue with the appropriate government investigators early in the process. The overriding goal in the early stages of a government investigation is to identify the concerns of the government and to demonstrate that the provider is taking the concerns and the investigation seriously.

Damaging Communication

Any document or type of contract, such as an employment agreement or service agreement, can lead to litigation or problems. More concerning in recent times are e-mails and internal memoranda sent within an organization with an unfound expectation of privacy. The language in such documents tends to be more casual, unlike a formal letter, and thus potentially more damaging. In recent years, there have been several high profile cases where internal e-mails have been effectively used against a company.

Advertising and Marketing Issues in Health Care

Under the anti-kickback statute it is improper for a hospital, for example, to provide any item of value to a physician in a position to refer federal health care program business to the hospital if the intent is to induce or reward such referrals. In the context of advertising, there are several issues to be aware of: (1) is the advertisement "something of value" to the physician, and (2) could the government argue that the advertisement was developed, and the participating physicians selected, in such a manner as to "induce" referrals from the physicians (or reward them for past referrals).

In a 2002 OIG Advisory Opinion, the OIG reconfirmed its general position on advertising and stated "advertising activity, like any marketing, implicates the anti-kickback statute because, by its nature, it is meant to recommend the use of a product." However, this broad statement does little except to indicate that advertising *could* raise issues. While there is little formal guidance on the proper means for a hospital (or other health care facility) to conduct advertising with physicians, there are a great number of cases where the government has prosecuted providers for indirect and direct kickback relationships whereby the physicians are rewarded in some way or another for directing business or referring business to a provider.

Marketing arrangements, separate from advertising, can also cause issues. For example, if a health care company retains someone to market its services and pays the person either on a per patient basis or based on volume, the compensation could be viewed as a kickback if the arrangement involves federal program patients.

Adjusting to the Legal Environment

Because the laws affecting health care providers are vast, complex, and oftentimes unintuitive, providers should obtain a sound foundation of knowledge about applicable health care laws in order that risks can be minimized and opportunities pursued. The following steps should be considered:

1. <u>Become Educated</u>. Depending on the size of your organization, you may not have the ability or resources to become an "expert" in all applicable areas of health law. Rather, pursue an alternative education track—attend seminars, read trade journals and Medicare and Medicaid publications, and search the government Web sites.
2. <u>Act in Good Faith.</u> A provider who has proceeded in good faith based on a proper and thorough investigation of the legal issues associated with his or her conduct will be in a good position to persuade a government agency or prosecutor against taking action if in fact a violation occurs.
3. <u>Seek Assistance when Necessary</u>. If you have "spotted the issue" and need further assistance (or if you do not know if an issue is present), obtain assistance from a qualified professional. Remember, be proactive!

Howard Bogard is a partner in the Birmingham, Alabama office of Burr & Forman LLP. Mr. Bogard's health law practice includes experience in Medicare and Medicaid fraud and abuse issues, Health Insurance Portability and Accountability Act compliance, health care regulatory compliance, facility licensure issues, patient rights, corporate compliance, and joint venture development. He represents hospitals, medical staffs, physician practices, nursing homes, diagnostic centers, and a variety of other health care providers and related associations and organizations.

Mr. Bogard earned his B.A. degree in history from the University of Florida in 1989 and his J.D. degree from Emory University School of Law in 1992. He is a co-author of The Legal Guide for Physicians *in Alabama and is a frequent speaker and author on a variety of health law topics. Mr. Bogard was admitted to the Alabama Bar in 1992 and the District of Columbia Bar in 1994, and is a member of the American and Birmingham Bar Associations, the American Health Lawyers Association, the Alabama and District of Columbia Health Law Practice Sections, and the American Bar Association forum committees on health and administrative law.*

Developing Legal Strategies in Health Care

Deane Kenworthy Corliss
Partner & Chair of Health Law Practice Group
Bradley Arant Rose & White LLP

An Overview

The health care industry is a very broad industry with many components. Most of my clients are service providers of one kind or another, such as hospitals, physicians, optometrists, and dentists, but of course they interact with the other components of the industry such as the pharmaceutical industry, medical device manufacturers, and various sorts of suppliers. To get paid for their work, they also have to interact with governmental payors (primarily Medicare and Medicaid), managed care payors such as HMOs, and other insurers. The business of the health care industry is complex, and so are the laws that regulate them. In the United States, the health care industry is one of the most heavily regulated industries, second only to the nuclear industry. Ultimately, these service providers exist to serve the public, to heal and to develop new ways of healing. But like every other business, they must be financially stable if they are to fulfill that mission. If they are to remain financially stable, they have to comply with the many laws that govern them, because failure to comply can result in huge fines and loss of the ability to be paid by the government for services.

When developing a legal strategy for my clients, the most important thing for me is to understand the dynamics of the client's particular business, to understand where that client fits in the jigsaw puzzle that is the health care industry, and to understand the particular stresses and strains of their business. I have to understand the technical side of what a client does, but I also have to understand the business and regulatory environment in which the client operates.

In legal representation of any business, it's important to understand the goals of the business for the immediate future and for long-term development, but in the health care industry it's absolutely vital to understand the dynamics of the referral patterns within their particular business, as well as the mechanisms by which they get paid. It's also important to understand what kinds of licenses and permits they need to conduct their business. All of those things affect the legal analysis of what the client wants to do.

The general public thinks one of the most important things that lawyers do in representing their clients is talking and arguing, and that's often a very important part of what a lawyer does for a client. But in my type of practice, one of the important things I do is listen, for what the client wants to do and for the nuances of the relationships with other components of the industry that could cause legal problems.

I am primarily a transactional and regulatory lawyer. I came from a background of nursing and public health, and I think of myself as a preventive kind of lawyer — one who tries to prevent my clients from violating the law, who tries to help guide their business relationships so they comply with the extremely complex laws that surround this industry, and one who helps them accomplish the transactions they want to accomplish within the bounds of those laws. To be able to accomplish that, I have to have a close working relationship with my clients. My practice is both transactional — for instance, structuring acquisitions or sales or joint ventures — and operational — dealing with the day-to-day issues of a health care provider.

My ultimate goal with my clients is to be in the role of a counselor. Attorneys used to be called "counselors." I want to be a trusted advisor, one they will call to help them think through what it is they want to do (before they go ahead and do it) and to keep them out of trouble.

That's the kind of relationship I really try to develop so my clients feel free to discuss their goals with me and let me help them structure their business relationships in a way I believe complies with the requirements of the law. I want to be part of the planning, so that the transaction is structured properly from the beginning. I also want to be part of the day-to-day problem solving and operations of my health care provider clients.

I am not a litigator. I think people who are litigators often have a different kind of relationship with their clients, because they come into the relationship when the client has already been sued. In that situation, another relationship the client has is already seriously broken, and the attorney is trying to help the client work their way out of that lawsuit. I prefer to be on the proactive side of things, and I try to structure relationships to prevent lawsuits either from private parties or from the government.

We all know business relationships can turn sour. Business partners can be the best of friends when a venture is formed, but years down the road the relationship can disintegrate. Part of what I do in the beginning of a business relationship is plan for what will happen to the ownership or relationship if the parties decide they no longer want to be associated with each other. Often, the original documents can be drafted to deal with the issues that will arise, so that if a "business divorce" occurs, at least the parties will know their respective rights in the assets of the business.

Much of the work I do for clients is the kind of work any business lawyer does — structuring transactions such as purchases and sales of businesses, structuring contractual relationships so the business can move forward with the infrastructure it needs, and various regulatory work. But because of the special types of laws that apply to the health care industry, underlying everything I do is a complex matrix of federal and state law that often dictates business terms.

As I'll discuss in more detail later, the laws regulating how health care providers are paid create a risk that the provider will be accused of false billings and other illegal practices associated with billing government programs, often referred to as "fraud and abuse." When providers are accused of these practices, whether by private parties or by the government, part of my practice involves investigation of the allegations, analysis of whether the allegations are true, and determination of whether the provider should settle the matter or defend vigorously. This part of my practice may involve collaboration with the firm's white-collar crime and health care fraud practice group.

There is another aspect to my work, and that is the patient care component. In every part of the health care industry, people are being served or cared for in one way or another, regardless of who or what the particular type of provider is. People, and their health care needs, are the reason for the existence of the health care industry. And despite the incredible technical advances in medical care, machines are simply the tools used to assist human beings in delivering health care to fellow human beings. As in all human relationships, there are opportunities for misunderstandings between the provider and patient. Sometimes, difficult ethical decisions must be made. Sometimes, there are bad outcomes from the care that is delivered. And sometimes, I am called upon to help providers figure out how to respond in those situations. I think my almost twenty years as a nurse helps to give me some insight into the dynamics of the relationship between the provider and their clients, and to help them respond appropriately.

I work with them on death and dying issues, sometimes helping providers understand not only the laws that govern, for instance, whether a family member can authorize the withdrawal of life support, but also the family dynamics that can affect those decisions. I work with them when a malpractice event has arguably occurred, for instance providing advice about whether an apology is advisable. I work with them on issues of patient consent to treatment, particularly where children are the patients, dealing with the relative rights of parents and children in making health care decisions. I work with them on medical staff credentialing, helping them sort through the complex issues that surround quality of care and the due process rights of physicians in medical staff credentialing. These are just some of the many issues that can occur on a daily basis as part of the operations of health care providers, people who are providing service to other people. As in all phases of my work, judgment and analysis of the law are required, but this type of work incorporates knowledge gained from my many years of being a clinician. That experience, and the personal knowledge of what it is like to be health care provider, enriches my analysis of the issues.

Legal Issues

The dynamics of the health care industry are very different from the dynamics involved in most other industries, such as manufacturing or even other types of non-health care service providers. There are two kinds of customers in the health care industry. One is the individual receiving health care, and the other is the insurance company paying for the care. In most other industries, the person receiving the goods or services pays for them directly, which creates natural incentives to keep consumption within one's economic means. But in the health care industry, a large part of the payment is by insurance that is either private like Blue Cross or a governmental program like Medicare or Medicaid. People pay premiums for their insurance, and their expectation is that the insurance will pay for any care they need, regardless of cost. For those who do not have any insurance coverage, or who are underinsured, there are issues of access to care, and when health care professionals and institutions do provide care to the medically indigent, either costs must be shifted to those who are insured or the provider must provide the care for free.

Fraud and Abuse

The economic dynamics of the health care industry create interesting dynamics in the legal world in which this industry functions. One of the most common legal issues I face in everything I do is a body of laws that stems from the way in which health care is paid for. Those laws are dominated by federal laws involving the Medicare and Medicaid reimbursement.

Because spending under the federal health care programs encompasses such a huge (and growing) part of the federal budget, Congress has for many years sought to restrict spending to care that is medically necessary, and to prevent fraud and abuse in the federal health care programs. Numerous laws and regulations have been enacted and promulgated, but there are three types of laws that affect almost every health care transaction and every day of operations of a health care provider.

First, there is the federal Anti-Kickback Statute. This is a very broad statute that prohibits remuneration in exchange for referrals. While it sounds like a very straightforward prohibition against bribes, it actually has been interpreted by the Office of Inspector General to be implicated in virtually every situation in which health care providers have any sort of payment relationship with referral sources. For instance, if a hospital enters into a contract with a physician to serve as a medical director, the statute is implicated. It is also implicated if a hospital wants to build a new facility as a joint venture with physicians on its medical staff. If an ambulance company wants to enter into a contract with the city to be its primary ambulance company and provide some sort of a discount, the statute is implicated. Violation of the Anti-Kickback Statute can be prosecuted criminally as a felony, leading to criminal fines and imprisonment, or it can be prosecuted administratively, leading to civil fines. In both cases, the provider can also be excluded from the Medicare and Medicaid programs — that is often called the "economic death penalty," because Medicare and Medicaid cover such a large number of people that many providers simply must be participants in those programs in order to remain economically viable.

Second, there is the federal law involving physician self-referral, commonly known as the "Stark Law." This law was enacted because Congress believed that when physicians have a financial relationship with entities to which they refer, their judgment about what is best for the patient may be skewed by their economic interest. The Stark Law prohibits referrals by physicians to entities with which they have a financial relationship (ownership or compensation). There are numerous exceptions to the law, and all relationships in which physicians have a financial relationship with entities to which they refer must be analyzed and shaped to conform to the exceptions.

There are also numerous laws and regulations that involve general billing compliance. For instance, these laws and regulations prohibit the submission of a bill for services that the provider knows are not medically necessary, they prohibit false statements in billing, and they prohibit certain activities that are designed to induce a patient to use a particular provider.

The economic penalties that are involved in violation of all of these laws are huge. They range from about $5,000 per claim to about $50,000 per claim. Because they are assessed on a per-claim basis, these penalties are often in the millions, and even hundreds of millions, of dollars.

The Federal False Claims Act is an additional means of policing false bills or requests to the federal government for payment in the health care delivery system. In part, the Federal False Claims Act imposes civil penalties on any person who knowingly presents a false claim to the federal government, knowingly makes a false statement to obtain payment, or conspires to defraud the federal government by having a false or fraudulent claim allowed or paid. The Federal False Claims Act was originally enacted to police false claims from military contractors during the Civil War, but after amendments in the 1980s, recoveries in the health care industry have by far outdistanced recoveries in the military context. This statute can be prosecuted not only by the federal government, but claims can also be brought by private "relators" on behalf of the federal government in "qui tam" actions. If the action is successful against the provider, the relator can share significantly in the monetary recovery. If a violation is proved, there are significant monetary penalties for each fraudulent claim, plus an amount equal to three times the amount of damages caused by each such claim. Penalties also include exclusion from the Medicare and Medicaid programs. Because of the per-claim penalties and the trebling of per-claim damages, like the other statutes noted above, penalties can be in the millions, or hundreds of millions, of dollars.

So how do providers avoid these problems? First, they have to have a corporate compliance program that makes sure there is adequate training of personnel. They have to do self-audits to discover billing problems. When they enter into financial relationships — from the simplest contract to the most complicated joint venture — they have to be sure the relationship has been analyzed by and structured by a competent health care attorney.

Corporate Governance

With enactment of the Sarbanes-Oxley Act, the federal government is placing greater emphasis on responsibility of corporate officers for adequate controls to prevent financial fraud. The Sarbanes-Oxley Act only applies to companies whose stock is publicly traded, but many of the principles of the act are prudent for non-publicly traded companies to adopt. In addition, principles of fiduciary duty of directors to oversee the activities of their companies are being reexamined in the courts, and health care companies are increasingly adopting corporate governance policies to help guide them to assure that there is an appropriate level of supervision from the board of directors to prevent health care fraud.

Nonprofit Companies

This body of laws deals with whether or not an entity pays federal income tax and state income tax — entities that are exempt from taxation are known as "nonprofits." The nonprofit sector of the health care industry is composed primarily of hospitals and some other institutional providers. Because tax-exempt status is so important to their functioning, it's very important that they comply with all the laws governing that status. They are prohibited from giving an excess private benefit to a private individual, or allowing their net profits to inure to the benefit of a private individual. An alternative to the draconian remedy of revocation of tax-exempt status is the imposition of "intermediate sanctions," or excise taxes on individuals who receive an excess private benefit and certain managers who participated in the decision.

There is a good deal of publicity right now about Congressional investigations into the way nonprofit entities conduct their business, especially their billing and collections practices. Congress is currently holding hearings on those kinds of practices, and there are a number of lawsuits around the country in which private individual class actions have been filed against nonprofit entities because of their billing and collection practices. There are numerous concerns, including failure of nonprofits in some cases to provide discounts to medically indigent uninsured patients and aggressive collection practices that have sometimes occurred. Hospitals are well advised to have policies regarding the amount and manner in which they will provide care to indigents, and to have adequate controls over their collection agencies to assure that overly aggressive collection practices do not occur.

Professional Standards

A third body of law concerns professional standards of practice, negligence, and medical malpractice When there is a bad outcome, it is not always the health care provider's fault; there are risks inherent in every medical procedure. But there are times when providers make mistakes, because providers are human. When that happens, the question people ask is, "Should the physician stiff arm the patient and keep them at a distance, or should they own up to being human and having made a mistake?" I prefer the latter approach in those situations, because I think that in most situations the patient simply wants to know the physician cares about them. They want recognition of their suffering and of the fact that the physician is human. And they want recognition that the physician is doing what he or she can to alleviate the patient's suffering, which is what people depend upon physicians to do.

Licensure

The next area in which we commonly see legal issues is the area of licensure, which is primarily a state law issue. Individuals who are health care providers usually must be licensed to perform their services; health care facilities frequently also have to be licensed. The licensure laws are specific to each profession and each facility. In the case of individuals, such as physicians, they involve the basic education and experience that someone must have to be licensed, the continuing education requirements, and various standards of professional conduct. In the case of health care facilities, they involve standards for the types of services that are conducted within the facility, the quality of staffing and construction, and other life safety code requirements. Threatened revocations of a professional's license to practice or a facility's license to operate are devastating events. Each licensing agency has its own rules for revocation and due process rights afforded the licensee.

Medical Staff Credentialing

Another area in which I am called upon to provide advice is medical staff credentialing. This is another thing that is very unusual about this particular industry. Professionals don't simply get to practice in any facility of their choice, such as a hospital. They have to meet criteria established by the hospital and its medical staff to be granted credentials as a member of the medical staff so they can practice at that facility, and they have to be granted specific privileges that govern the scope of the services they can perform in the facility. This process is designed to assure that the professionals have adequate skills to conduct their practices, and those credentials and privileges can be taken away if there are issues of quality.

The question often arises in those situations as to whether or not there really is an issue of quality, or whether there is actually a competitive issue where medical staff members are trying to keep a competitor from getting on the medical staff or trying to kick somebody off because they don't want them to be able to compete.

Professionals whose privileges are revoked or restricted sometimes sue the people who participated in the process, claiming that the decision was based on competitive issues rather than on quality concerns. Often, the professional is seeking redress under the antitrust laws that have a treble damages aspect to them, so there is a real monetary incentive for that professional to try to use that theory in the lawsuit. The claims often include defamation and interference with business relations, which in a successful lawsuit can result in punitive damages, another monetary incentive to sue. For instance, a way of calculating that would be, if a physician loses medical staff privileges and is no longer able to practice his or her profession in that town, because it's a one-hospital town, that physician is going to claim, "I made $200,000 last year when I was practicing. My damages are the loss of my income for the remaining years of my practice times three." That monetary incentive is why antitrust claims are a fairly common component in these types of lawsuits.

There are numerous protections that are available to professionals as part of the credentialing process. Medicare and the accrediting agencies require facilities to have due process rights for professionals in credentialing and peer review actions. These due process rights involve notice, hearing, and opportunity to present their own case before a hearing committee or hearing officer. For health care institutions and people who participate in peer review proceedings, there is a federal law that provides immunity for the health care institution and the people who participate in good faith peer review actions. This law was passed in 1986, because Congress recognized that peer review activity is for the benefit of the public. It wanted to encourage good faith peer review and protect people who participate in good faith peer review from lawsuits.

Privacy and Security of Health Information

The Health Insurance Portability and Accountability Act, better known as HIPAA, is a vast law. One part of it deals with portability and continuation of health care insurance, and whether a job change can trigger waiting periods and exclusion for preexisting conditions. Another part required either the statutory or regulatory promulgation of standards protecting the privacy and security of health care information. The regulations affecting the privacy of health care information went into effect in the spring of 2003. The regulations affecting the security of health care information will go into effect in April of 2005. These regulations result in large part from concerns about the way health care information is handled and transmitted, because so much information is now transmitted electronically or housed in computers. These standards are complex and detailed; while providers have traditionally known there is a need to maintain confidentiality and security of medical information, as a result of the HIPAA privacy and security standards, providers have had to institute numerous procedures and safeguards to comply with the standards. They frequently need legal help to understand their obligations, draft the policies, and implement the procedures.

Steps to Avoid Legal Problems

If I had to summarize in one word the steps health care providers can take to avoid legal problems, I would say, "planning." If health care providers and health care institutions would step back a moment and think about the kinds of behaviors that get them into legal trouble most often, and then try to take steps to prevent those behaviors from happening, they could avoid many legal problems.

In the health care industry, the planning process often involves having a corporate compliance plan. It defines certain codes of conduct and then implements processes to assure that the institution and its employees comply with the code of conduct. Institutional providers such as hospitals are well aware that a corporate compliance plan is essential to their functioning, but even small physician practices would benefit from having a compliance plan.

A close relationship with the provider's legal advisor can help prevent legal problems as well. That may sound self-serving, but it has been my experience that providers can avoid the huge costs of litigation by consulting their legal advisors before beginning their business deals, rather than jumping into them and finding out the pitfalls of the relationship later.

Emerging Issues in Health Care Law

Employers and the federal government are continually seeking ways to limit the exponential increase in health care costs. One result of those efforts is that reimbursement to providers, especially physicians, is not keeping up with cost increases to those providers. Physicians have increasingly been seeking ways to augment their income by investing in various types of health care facilities. While the Stark Law places numerous constraints on those investments, it currently allows physicians to refer to a few types of entities in which they have an investment interest, such as ambulatory surgery centers. The result is that there are an increasing number of physician-owned facilities being built across the nation, often in a joint venture with a nearby hospital. This trend is expected to continue. There are many legal challenges in structuring some of these joint ventures, including not only the Stark Law, but also the Anti-Kickback Statute and laws governing nonprofit entities.

As the population ages and more baby boomers approach the age of eligibility for Medicare, Congress has become increasingly concerned about expenditures for health care under the Medicare and Medicaid programs. The result, in part, has been the enactment of or increased enforcement of laws designed to prevent fraud and abuse against the federal health care programs. Health lawyers in recent years have spent an increasing amount of their time and effort helping clients respond to governmental investigations and qui tam actions, and this trend is expected to continue.

E-law is another body of law and practice that is developing. Some members of Congress and the administration that controls the Medicare program (the Centers for Medicare and Medicaid Administration, or CMS) have expressed a desire to develop a truly electronic medical record. An electronic medical record would allow access to a provider anywhere. It would, for example, facilitate care if someone were traveling outside his or her state of residence, because it would allow the provider to access the medical record located in the state of residence. This concept has the potential for Orwellian problems, but it also has the potential for a great deal of good. The issues associated with the security of the health information being transmitted and the integrity of that information are addressed in the HIPAA security standards, which must be implemented for most providers by April of 2005. However, a truly massive, national medical record system is very different from an electronic medical record that is kept within the confines of a hospital's walls, accessible only to its medical staff and employees. Obviously, there will be many safeguards that would have to be implemented before a national medical record could be considered secure. The concept also raises concerns about unauthorized access to medical information, particularly by the government.

Ethical issues in the delivery of health care continue to develop, particularly with respect to research, such as research on stem cells derived from fetal tissue. As organ and other tissue transplant techniques develop, and particularly as drugs to suppress rejection are developed, we can expect more issues to arise related to obtaining organs from both living donors and cadaveric donors.

When Litigation is Necessary

Ending up in court and ending up with a lawsuit are actually, in my mind, two different things, because people seem to file lawsuits pretty liberally, but most of those lawsuits never make it to trial. Generally, only about 10 percent of filed lawsuits end up going to trial. Sometimes, lawsuits are filed in an effort to gain a negotiating advantage.

Lawsuits certainly arise in situations other than malpractice. There are many that arise as pure business disputes in the health care industry. Remember that this is a very big industry, with many different components. It involves a number of different kinds of providers, and those providers often have business disputes with each other. For instance, physicians who are in practice together may end up hating each other and decide they have to get the equivalent of a divorce. If they can't reconcile their economic differences, they may end up in a lawsuit — and often the one who files is merely trying to gain a negotiating advantage over the other.

Other cases may be brought by the government, claiming that a provider has violated the Stark Law, or the Anti-Kickback Statute, or has filed false claims. As I mentioned before, some of these cases may be brought by a relator in a qui tam action. In these cases, an individual whistle blower brings a case under the Federal False Claims Act on behalf of the government; if the claim is successful, the relator receives a large portion of the damage award.

Once litigation occurs, I think close communication with the attorney who is handling the dispute is very important. Clients should provide the attorney with adequate background information and be open and honest about what occurred. Hiding information from the attorney, or putting the situation only in the best light, will not be helpful in winning the case. A close, cooperative working relationship is the best bet you have for a good outcome.

Deane Kenworthy Corliss is chair of the health care practice group of Bradley Arant Rose & White LLP. She represents virtually all types of health care providers, from the smallest of physician practices to some of the largest hospital systems in Alabama.

Her practice is both transactional and operational. Her transactional experience includes acquisitions and sales of hospital systems and physician practices, as well as formation of joint ventures among for-profit and nonprofit entities. Her operational practice includes analysis of Stark and fraud and abuse laws in a variety of relationships, investigation of fraud and abuse allegations, and she is frequently asked to advise other general practice attorneys on these issues. Corporate governance, corporate compliance, HIPAA privacy compliance, contracting, medical staff issues, and risk management are all part of her daily practice. Many of her clients are nonprofit entities, and she regularly advises them on intermediate sanctions and inurnment issues. When expertise in health law is required, she assists the firm's white-collar crime and health care fraud practice groups.